The flowering plants of South Africa vol. 2

By

I. B. Pole Evans

PUBLISHED BY: 2024 by BTB Publishing

ISBN : 978-1-63652-369-9

THE FLOWERING PLANTS OF SOUTH AFRICA

VOL. 2

I. B. POLE EVANS

CONTENTS

K. A. LANSDELL DEL.

PLATE 41.

ALOE WICKENSII.
Transvaal.

LILIACEAE. TRIBE ALOINEAE.

ALOE, Linn.; Benth. et Hook. f. Gen. Plant.
Aloe Wickensii, *Pole Evans in Trans. Roy. Soc. S. Afr.*

This is one of the most beautiful and showy of the South Africa species of *Aloe*. Specimens were collected by Messrs. Wickens and Pienaar in M'Phathlele's Location in the Northern Transvaal, in January, 1914. The species is also found widely distributed in the Oliphants River Bushveld. It is now established in the Garden of the Division of Botany, Pretoria, and in the latter part of July and August when in flower is a source of great admiration to visitors.

In general appearance and habit of growth this *Aloe* closely resembles *A. Pienaarii* from the same locality, figured in vol. i. of this work (Plate 27), but it is more commonly found on gentle slopes in bush country, although it may frequently occur in open ground along with *A. Pienaarii*. When the plants are not in flower, those of *A. Wickensii* can be distinguished from *A. Pienaarii* by their paler green leaves, which are distinctly incurved.

We propose the name "Wickens' Aloe" for this species.

Specimens are preserved in the National Herbarium, Pretoria (Herb. No. 1449).

DESCRIPTION:—A stemless succulent herb. *Leaves* pale glaucous-green, 40-50 in a dense rosette, 50-70 cm. long, 10-13 cm. broad at the base, lanceolate-ensiform, erect, distinctly incurved, rather flat above, convex beneath, beset on the margins with small deltoid black prickles about 2 mm. long and about 6-8 mm. apart. *Inflorescences* often 2-4 from the same rosette, spreading. *Peduncle* laterally compressed, naked, with usually two lateral branches, branches arcuateerect, clothed with pale brown scariose broadly ovate-acuminate bracts. *Raceme* dense-flowered, 17-20 cm. long, conical-cylindric. *Bracts* reflexed, 5-6 mm. long, ovate-cuspidate, scariose, pellucid. *Pedicels* recurved, 3-4 mm. long. *Perianth* 3·5 cm. long, cylindric-ventricose; outer segments free for 16-17 mm., obtuse and recurved at the apex, 3-5-nerved; inner segments obtuse and recurved, 3-nerved. *Stamens* projecting 11 mm. beyond the perianth and slightly recurved. *Style* stout, strongly recurved. *Fruit* 2·5 cm. long, 1·3 cm. in diameter, oblong-ovoid.

PLATE 41.—Fig. 1, entire plant, much reduced; Fig. 2, raceme; Fig. 3, portion of leaf; Fig. 4, transverse section of leaf; Fig. 5, bract; Fig. 6, open flower; Fig. 7, fruit showing remains of perianth attached.

F.P.S.A., 1922.

M. PAGE DEL.

PLATE 42.

COMMELINA BENGHALENSIS.
Cape Province, Natal, Transvaal.

COMMELINACEAE. TRIBE COMMELINEAE.

COMMELINA, Linn.; Benth. et Hook. f. Gen. Plant.
Commelina benghalensis, *Linn. Sp. Pl. 41; Fl.*

A common species in certain habitats in South Africa, and extending to Tropical Africa, throughout India to Japan, and the Moluccas. On account of its easy cultivation and the exquisite deep shade of blue of the petals, it deserves more recognition from gardeners, and should be at least as great a favourite as species of *Tradescantia* (The Wandering Jew). The floral structure shows interesting modifications in the stamens, and a study of the method of pollination would certainly bring to light some interesting facts. This plant often produces at the base modified (cleistogamic) flowers which burrow into the ground and produce small capsules.

The original drawing from which our figure has been reproduced was prepared by Miss Page and loaned by the Curator of the Bolus Herbarium. The plants flowered in March and April at the National Botanic Gardens, Kirstenbosch (No. 1232/18), and were sent by Mr. G. Hay from Louis Trichardt, Transvaal.

DESCRIPTION:—A diffuse herbaceous plant. *Stem* 15-80 cm. long. *Leaves* 3-8 cm. long, 1·5-3·5 cm. broad, ovate or elliptic-ovate, acute, contracted at the base into a sheath often ciliate with reddish hairs, and usually wavy margins. *Flowers* partly enclosed in a green hairy spathe, the topmost flower long-exserted. *Sepals* 3; the two side sepals more or less orbicular; the odd sepal elliptic. *Petals* 3; the two side petals dark blue, semi-orbicular, produced at the base into a distinct claw; the odd petal small, ovate-elliptic. *Stamens* 6, divided into three sets; three stamens barren, forming staminodes; the three side stamens blue; one stamen yellow, with two appendages at the back of the anther. *Ovary* sub-globose, 3-celled; style cylindric; stigma simple. *Fruit* obovoid, 3-celled. *Seeds* more or less oblong, wrinkled.

PLATE 42.—Fig. 1, inflorescence in bud; Fig. 2, the same with half of spathe removed; Fig. 3, side sepal × 2; Fig. 4, odd sepal × 2; Fig. 5, side petal × 2; Fig. 6, odd petal × 2; Fig. 7, stamens and pistil × 3; Fig. 8, small anther (blue) × 5; Figs. 9, 10, larger anthers (yellow), front and back view × 5; Fig. 11, fruit × 4; Fig. 12, transverse section of fruit; Fig. 13, seed, enlarged.

F.P.S.A., 1922.

M. PAGE DEL.

PLATE 43.

HESSEA Zeyheri.
Cape Province, Little Namaqualand.

Amaryllidaceae. Tribe Amaryllideae.

Hessea, Herb.; Benth. et Hook. f. Gen. Plant.
Hessea Zeyheri, *Baker, Handb. Amaryllid. p. 23; Fl. Cap.*

This is a very rare species here figured for the first time. It was discovered by Carl Zeyher at Hardeveld in little Namaqualand about the year 1847, and appears to have been unrecorded since then until recently collected by Mr. E. B. Watermeyer. The genus *Hessea* is endemic to South Africa, and contains nine species found in the Cape Province, Little Namaqualand, and one species from the Transvaal. Hitherto none has been recorded from Natal or the Orange Free State. Our specimen differs slightly from the original described in the "Flora Capensis" in having three rather shorter leaves contemporary with the flowers. At first the style is short, but elongates as the flowers mature.

Our illustration was prepared from a drawing by Miss M. Page of specimens which flowered in April at the National Botanic Gardens, Kirstenbosch (No. 1157/16), and collected by Mr. E. B. Watermeyer, Nieuwoudtville, Calvinia Division. The drawing has been kindly loaned by the Curator of the Bolus Herbarium.

Description:—*Bulb* 5 cm. long, 3·5 cm. in diameter, sub-globose, produced above into a short neck. *Leaves* 3, contemporary with the flowers, 5·5-11·5 cm. long, 0·8-16 cm. broad, strap-shaped, obtuse, narrowing and channelled at the base. *Peduncle* arising at the side of the leaves, about 10 cm. long, flattened. *Spathe-valves* 2 cm. long, linear, acuminate. *Inflorescence* an umbel of about 25 flowers. *Pedicels* 2-3 cm. long. *Perianth tube* 3 mm. long; segments about 1 cm. long, oblong-lanceolate, obtuse, united to the staminal tube by the midrib. *Stamens* of two different lengths, the filaments united below into a tube 4 mm. long; free portions of filaments 8 mm. and 5 mm. long; anthers of long stamens globose, of short stamens oblong. *Ovary* 1·6 mm. in diameter, globose; style short in bud, lengthening to 15 mm. in older flowers.

PLATE 43.—Fig. 1, section through perianth × 3; Fig. 2, lobe of perianth × 3.

F.P.S.A., 1922.

K. A. LANSDELL DEL.

PLATE 44.

CEROPEGIA TRISTIS.
Cape Province, Natal.

ASCLEPIADACEAE. TRIBE CEROPEGIEAE.

CEROPEGIA, *Linn.; Benth. et Hook. f. Gen. Plant.*

Ceropegia tristis, *Hutchinson*, sp. nov.; affinis *C. Haygarthii*, Schlechter, sed foliis sub anthesi bene evolutis, calyce majori, corollae lobis brevissime stipitatis differt.

Scandens; caulis carnosus, glaber. *Folia* breviter petiolata matura 3·5-6 cm. longa, 1·5-3·5 cm. lata, late oblonga vel oblongo-ovata, apice breviter apiculata, basi cordata, glabra; nervi laterales utrinsecus circiter 4, patuli; petioli circiter 1 cm. longi. *Cymae* axillares, triflorae; pedicelii usque ad 1·5 cm. longi, teretes, glabri. *Sepala* lineari-filiformia, 3-4 mm. longa, glabra, marginibus leviter hyalinis. *Corolla* basi subglobosa, supra basin curvato-erecta, circiter 6 cm. longa, superne turbinata, apice 2 cm. diametro, extra glabra, maculata, intra leviter pilosa, lobis e basi lata attenuatis in columnam brevem cohaerentibus, deinde apice corpusculam globosam 5-fenestratum ciliatam formantibus. *Corona* exterior cupularis, lobis 5 latis emarginatis columna staminalis sequilonga intra pilis longis gracilibus ciliatis; corona interior erecta, lobis conniventibus apice recurvatis. *Follicula* circiter 14 cm. longa, falcato-recurvata, apice sub-uncinata.—J. H.

In our last number (Plate 39) we figured a species of *Ceropegia Rendallii*, which belongs to a group of the genus characterised by having the corolla-lobes united into an umbrella-like canopy supported by five short stalks. The present species has the corolla-lobes free at the base, then connate into a slender column, again becoming free and then connate at the tips, forming a small terminal cage-like body.

It shares this character with *Ceropegia Haygarthii*, Schlechter, and in this respect the two species are unique amongst the South African species. In *C. Haygarthii*, however, the corolla is very widely globose at the base, the calyx lobes are longer, and the peculiar stalk to the corolla lobes is at least three or four times as long. These differences seem to warrant the description of a new species. The curiously shaped flowers should make this species an object of interest in the greenhouse.

DESCRIPTION:—A climber. *Stem* fleshy, glabrous. *Leaves* shortly petioled, 3·5-6 cm. long, 1·5-3·5 cm. broad, broadly oblong or oblong-ovate, apex rounded and shortly pointed, cordate at the base, glabrous; lateral nerves about four on each side; petiole about 1 cm. long. *Inflorescence* a 1-3-flowered axillary cyme; pedicels 1·2-1·5 cm. long, terete, glabrous. *Sepals* 4-5 mm. long, subulate, glabrous. *Corolla* abruptly bent at a right angle near the base; tube (following the bend) 2·6 cm. long, globosely inflated at the base, widening upwards and about 2 cm. in diameter at the mouth, glabrous without, finely pilose within; lobes free at the base, abruptly inflexed over the mouth of the tube and produced beneath into broad triangular partition-like green plates or keels, meeting at the centre and connate into a slender erect column about 2-3 mm. long, then again becoming free and expanding into elliptic-lanceolate replicate segments, connate at the tips, forming a small apical ellipsoid cage-like body, 5-8 mm.

long, ciliate on the margins. *Outer corona* cupular, with five broad emarginate lobes arising to the level of the staminal column, ciliate and hairy within with long fine hairs; inner corona lobes about 2·5 mm. long, linear, connivent-erect over the staminal column, with revolute tips. *Follicles* about 14 cm. long, strongly falcate, recurved at the tips.

PLATE 44.—Fig. 1, portion of stem with leaves and flowers, nat. size; Fig. 2, calyx; Fig. 3, lobe of corolla; Fig. 4, outer and inner corona; Fig. 5, staminal column; Fig. 6, pollinia; Fig. 7, follicles, nat. size. All enlarged with the exceptions of Figs. 1 and 7.

F.P.S.A., 1922.

4.5.

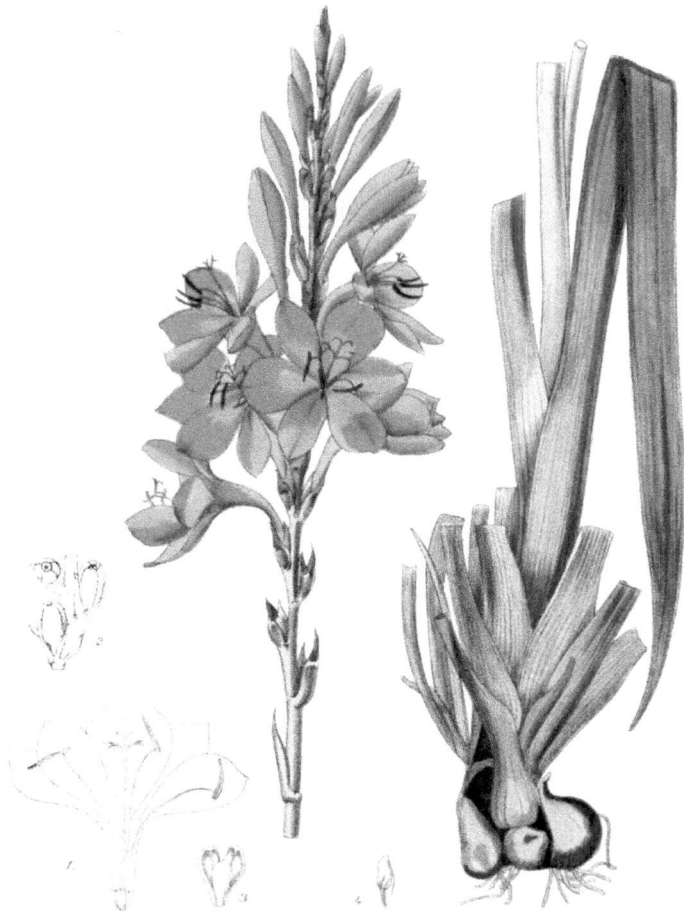

M. PAGE DEL.

PLATE 45.

WATSONIA GALPINII.
Cape Province.

IRIDACEAE. TRIBE IXIEAE.

WATSONIA, Mill.; Benth. et Hook. f. Gen. Plant.
Watsonia Galpinii, *L. Bolus. Ann. Bolus Herb.*

We have pleasure in figuring in this number, through the kindness of the Curator of the Bolus Herbarium, our first species of one of the most popular of South African genera, namely, *Watsonia.* Species of this genus have long been known in European Gardens, where they were introduced by the early botanical collectors from the Cape. The genus is represented in South Africa by about twenty species, and with the exception of a species which occurs in Madagascar, are confined to the sub-continent. The Watsonias lend themselves to hybridising, and some very fine garden hybrids have been produced.

The species here figured was first discovered by Mr. E. E. Galpin at Lottering Bush, Zitzikama (*Galpin* No. 4698), and re-collected at Knysna by Miss A. V. Duthie, who sent corms to the National Botanic Gardens, where they flowered in March, 1919 (No. 239/18).

The general name of "pijpie" is applied to almost all species of *Watsonia* and also to some species of *Gladiolus.*

DESCRIPTION:—*Corm* 2 cm. in diameter, depressed-globose, oblique at the base. *Stem* 75 cm. long, racemose. *Leaves* 4-8, radical, up to 35 cm. long, 1-1·5 cm. broad, linear, acute, acuminate, with the median and marginal nerves somewhat subprominent. *Inflorescence* simple or branched. *Spathe-valves* herbaceous or submembranous at the apex; the outer 0·6-3·2 cm. long, lanceolate, setaceous acuminate; the inner 0·8-1·4 cm. long, ovate or broadly ovate, acuminate. *Perianth-tube* 2 cm. long, constricted about the middle; the lower half filiform, scarcely 1·5 mm. in diameter; the upper half infundibuliform, 7 mm. in diameter near the throat; lobes spreading, 1·5 cm. long; the outer up to 8 mm. broad, suboblong, subacute, minutely apiculate; the inner 1 cm. broad, oblong-obovate. *Stamens* almost as long as the perianth lobes; anthers 9 mm. long. *Ovary* about 5 mm. long, subobconic; style 2·9 cm. long; primary branches 9 mm. long; stigmas about 2 mm. long. *Fruit* 1 cm. long, obconic.

Mrs. Bolus remarks, "Distinguished from the rest of the section 'Eu-Watsonia' by the more slender habit, the smaller spathe-valves, the shorter perianth-tube and relatively long segments."

PLATE 45.—Fig. 1, flower, perianth laid open; Fig. 2, portion of fruiting spike; Fig. 3, capsule, dehisced, about natural size; Fig. 4, seed × 2.

F.P.S.A., 1922.

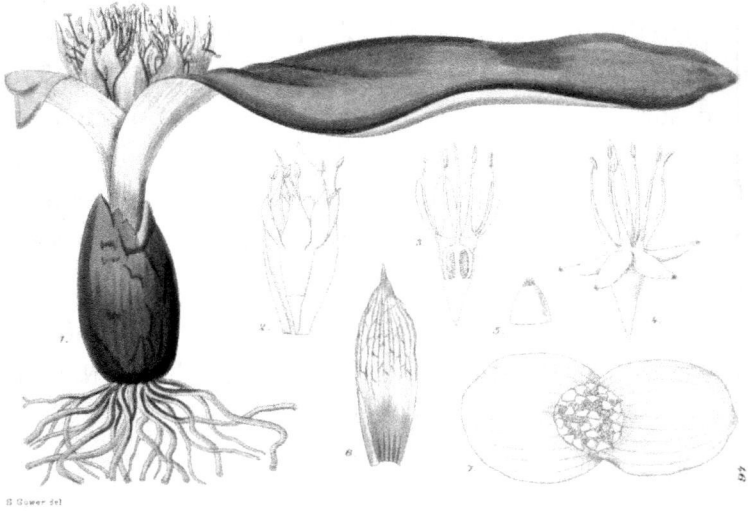

S. GOWER DEL.

PLATE 46.

MASSONIA LATIFOLIA.
Cape Province, Little Namaqualand.

Liliaceae. Tribe Allieae.

Massonia, Thunb.; Benth. et Hook. f. Gen. Plant.
Massonia latifolia, *Linn. fil. Suppl. 193; Fl.*

All the species of *Massonia*, an endemic Cape genus of the *Liliaceae*, have fragrant hyacinthoid flowers, arising in a sessile cluster from between two broad prostrate leaves. The name was given to the genus by Carl Thunberg to commemorate the name of Francis Masson, who was sent to the Cape in 1772 as collector for the Royal Gardens at Kew, and who was responsible for introducing a large number of Cape plants into cultivation. The first 20 volumes of Curtis's *Botanical Magazine*, which contain 786 plates, have nearly one-third devoted to figures of Cape species, mostly sent to Kew Gardens by Masson.

The genus *Massonia* is very imperfectly known, as about 24 out of the 33 species described in the "Flora Capensis" have never been collected within the last 50 years, or are only known from figures in botanical publications. It is, therefore, with some pleasure that we publish our first plate representing a species of the genus, collected by Mrs. E. Rood, of Van Rhynsdorp, in the hope that it may stimulate others to forward specimens to the Division of Botany, Pretoria, for illustration in future numbers of this work.

This particular species was figured by Jacquin in 1803.

Specimens are preserved in the National Herbarium, Pretoria (Herb. No. 1450).

DESCRIPTION:—*Bulb* 3·5 cm. long, 3 cm. broad, ovoid-ellipsoid, with brown membranous tunics. *Leaves* 2, lying flat on the ground, somewhat fleshy, 12 cm. long, 14·5 cm. broad, somewhat orbicular, narrowed and channelled at the base, glabrous. *Inflorescence* an abbreviated raceme. *Bracts* 3·5 cm. long, 1 cm. broad, lanceolate, acuminate, acute, about 5-nerved, glabrous. *Pedicels* 6 mm. long, 4 mm. broad, fleshy. *Perianth-tube* 7 mm. long, 6 mm. in diameter at the throat; lobes 1·2 mm. long, 4 mm. broad, oblong, minutely tufted at the apex, membranous. *Filaments* inserted at mouth of perianth-tube, 1·4 cm. long, ovate and connate at the base, becoming linear above; anthers 3 mm. long, linear, versatile. *Ovary* 5 mm. long, 7 mm. in diameter above, obovoid; style 2 cm. long, subterete; stigma simple.

PLATE 46.—Fig. 1, plant viewed from eye-level; Fig. 2, bract with flower; Fig. 3, section of flower; Fig. 4, flower, showing the filaments connate at the base; Fig. 5, apex of perianth lobe; Fig. 6, bract; Fig. 7, plant viewed from above. All enlarged with the exception of Figs. 1 and 7.

F.P.S.A., 1922.

47

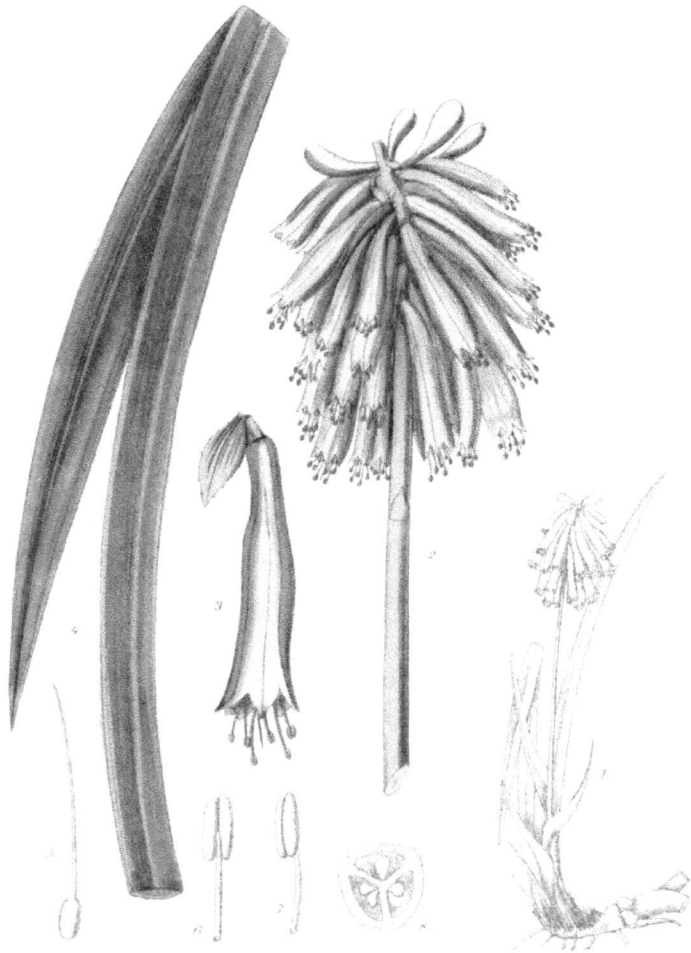

K. A. LANSDELL DEL.

PLATE 47.

KNIPHOFIA ALOOIDES.
Cape Province, Orange Free State, Transvaal, Basutoland, Natal.

LILIACEAE. TRIBE HEMEROCALLEAE.

KNIPHOFIA, Moench.; Benth. et Hook. f. Gen. Plant.
Kniphofia alooides, *Moench. Meth. 632; Fl. Cap.*
vol. vi. p. 283. Tritoma Uvaria, Gawl. in Bot. Mag. t.
758; Kniphofia Uvaria, Hook. Bot. Mag. t. 4816.

We may perhaps be excused for figuring this species, which has appeared as a plate more than once in Curtis's *Botanical Magazine*. It is, however, still such a favourite with cultivators that it is deemed worthy of a figure in a South African publication. Like other of our native plants it was known in European gardens many years ago, and is recorded as having flowered at Kew Gardens in 1707. As a cultivated plant it was known under the name of *Tritoma Uvaria*, which was later changed to *Kniphofia Uvaria*. It was also described by Linnaeus about the year 1735 as an *Aloe*. Specimens of the plant in cultivation may be seen in many South African gardens. It is the most robust and most variable species of the genus. In the coastal districts of Natal two varieties, *nobilis* and *maxima*, are found, but our figure and description apply to the typical form. The common name is the "Red-hot poker." The natives of Natal know the plant as "i-Cacane."

The plate was drawn from a specimen collected near Durban in July, 1914.

DESCRIPTION:—A perennial stemless plant with radical leaves,

20

and long naked peduncles, bearing a short spike of flowers at their apices. *Rootstock* thickened, not tuberous. *Leaves* 30-45 cm. long, 1·5-1·8 cm. broad low down, strap-shaped, acuminate, sheathing at the base, green, strongly and acutely keeled, with smooth margins. *Peduncle* a little shorter than the leaves, terete. *Inflorescence* 5 cm. long, dense, more or less cylindric. *Bracts* 0·3-1·2 cm. long, 3-6 mm. broad, ovate, obtuse or acute. *Perianth-tube* 3-4 cm. long, 5 mm. in diameter at the throat, more or less cylindric, 6-veined; lobes 2 mm. long, ovate, obtuse. *Stamens* 6, not all lengthening at the same time, exserted in the lower flowers. *Ovary* 3-celled, with many (12 or more) ovules in each cell; style exserted in the lower flowers; stigma obtuse.

PLATE 47.—Fig. 1, plant, reduced; Fig. 2, inflorescence; Fig. 3, flower with subtending bract; Fig. 4, leaf; Fig. 6, gynaecium; Figs. 6 and 7, stamens, front and back view; Fig. 8, cross-section through the ovary.

F.P.S.A., 1922.

K. A. LANSDELL DEL.

PLATE 48.

HELIOPHILA SCANDENS.
Natal.

CRUCIFERAE. TRIBE SISYMBRIEAE.

HELIOPHILA, Linn.; Benth. et Hook. Gen. Plant.
Heliophila Scandens, *Harv. Thes.*

Harvey first described and figured this remarkable species of *Heliophila* in 1863, from specimens which he received from Mr. M'Ken. The late Dr. Medley Wood sent a plant of it to Kew in 1885, which flowered in the succulent house the following year, and has continued to do so about mid-winter ever since. From the plant which flowered at Kew a plate was prepared for the *Botanical Magazine*, t. 7668.

According to the Kew authorities, in the whole of the large Natural Order *Cruciferae*, embracing about 180 genera, only two are recorded as having scandent species. They are the South African *Heliophila* and the Peruvian *Cremolobus*, and the scandent habit is exceptional in these two genera.

The plant may be found in shady places amongst shrubs along the coast near Durban and also at Inanda. The present plate was prepared from specimens gathered near Durban in July, 1914. The species is popularly known as the "Bridal Wreath."

DESCRIPTION:—A climbing plant. *Stem* brown; branches green, terete, glabrous. *Leaves* 2·5-5 cm. long, 1·2-2·5 cm. broad, oblong to lanceolate, tapering at both ends, obtuse or acute, gradually passing into a thickened, channelled and usually recurved petiole, glabrous. *Flowers* in axillary and terminal racemes; pedicels 1·2-2·5 cm. long. *Sepals* oblong, obtuse; the two lateral ones with thickened dorsal wings. *Petals* 0·8-1·2 cm. long, obovate-spathulate. *Long stamens* half as long as the petals; short stamens 4 mm. long; anthers ovate. *Ovary* globose; style short; stigma capitate. *Fruit* 4-5 cm. long, elliptic-oblong, flat, tipped by a short straight style, 1-2-seeded.

PLATE 48.—Fig. 1, portion of plant, nat. size; Fig. 2, flower; Figs. 3, 4, and 5, stamens; Fig. 6, petal; Fig. 7, gynaecium; Fig. 8, fruit. All enlarged with the exception of Fig. 1.

F.P.S.A., 1922.

K. A. Lansdell del

K. A. LANSDELL DEL.

PLATE 49.

Verbenaceae. Tribe Viticeae.

Holmskioldia, Retz.; Benth. et Hook. f. Gen. Plant.
Holmskioldia speciosa, *Hutchinson et Corbishley in Kew Bull. 1920.*

This beautiful and showy plant was first collected by Dr. I. B. Pole Evans at Komati Poort in November, 1917, and specimens sent to Kew were reported to be an undescribed species of the genus. Sir Wm. Hoy, the General Manager of the South African Railways, presented two living specimens to the Division of Botany, Pretoria, and our plate was prepared from these plants when they flowered.

The plant is a large bush 10-20 ft. high, and when in full bloom is one of the most conspicuous objects in the veld. The calyx in this species very soon becomes almost fully developed, and the young corolla is at first only visible as a minute ball at the base of the saucer-shaped calyx.

Holmskioldia is a small genus with a curious distribution. A handsome species, *H. sanguinea*, Retz, occurs in the foothills of the Himalaya mountains of India at an altitude of 3000-5000 ft. *H. tettensis*, *H. spinescens*, and *H. mucronata*, Vatke, are found in the basin of the Lower Zambesi and Shire Rivers, and there is an unnamed species in Madagascar. The genus is very closely related to *Clerodendron*, largely represented in all these areas.

Description:—*Branchlets* woody, terete, shortly and softly

pubescent, marked with pale lenticels; internodes about 2 cm. long. *Leaves* broadly ovate, triangular at the apex, broadly wedge-shaped at the base, 2·5-4 cm. long, 2-3 cm. broad, coarsely crenate, with few (about three) rounded teeth, very shortly setulose above, paler below and conspicuously glandular and shortly pubescent; lateral nerves about three on each side of the midrib; petiole 7 mm. long, densely pubescent. *Flowers* few, arranged in axillary cymes about 4 cm. long; peduncles slender, softly pubescent; lower bracts more or less leafy, spathulate-obovate, up to 7 mm. long; pedicels up to 1·2 cm. long, with two small opposite linear bracteoles above the middle. *Calyx* pink-coloured, gradually enlarging, broadly top-shaped, glandular-pubescent outside; tube 1 cm. long, with broadly rounded lobes, the latter rigidly membranous in the fruiting stage and expanding to 2·5 cm. *Corolla* purple, 2-2·5 cm. long, glandular and softly pubescent outside; tube up to 1·5 cm. long. *Stamens* long exserted; filaments glabrous. *Ovary* hairy in the upper part; style a little longer than the stamens, slender, glabrous. *Fruit* truncate, 4-horned, included by the accrescent calyx.—J. HUTCHINSON.

PLATE 49.—Fig. 1, calyx; Fig. 2, corolla bud; Fig. 3, stamen; Fig. 4, pistil; Fig. 5, young fruit.

F.P.S.A., 1922.

K. A. LANSDELL DEL.

PLATE 50.

SCROPHULARIACEAE. TRIBE GERARDIEAE.

RHAMPHICARPA, Benth.; Benth. et Hook. f. Gen. Plant.
Rhamphicarpa tubulosa, *Benth. in Hook.*
Comp. Bot. Mag. i. 368; Harv. Thes.

This species belongs to a small genus of plants which are probably parasitic or semi-parasitic herbs. Three species are known in South Africa, and a few from Tropical Africa, East India, and Australia. *R. tubulosa* also occurs in Tropical, and is the most widely distributed member of the genus in South Africa. In Natal it is always found in moist ground, edges of pools, and similar habitats.

The plate was prepared from plants collected by the late Dr. Medley Wood on the Berea Flats near Durban, Natal.

DESCRIPTION:—A herbaceous plant 12-60 cm. high. *Stem* erect; simple or occasionally sparsely branched, terete, sometimes furrowed on two sides, glabrous or nearly so. *Leaves* opposite or subopposite, exstipulate, sessile or nearly so, 2·6-7·5 cm. long, up to 1·2 cm. broad, linear, slightly narrowed at both ends, with entire margins and a prominent midrib, glabrous. *Inflorescence* a few-flowered raceme; pedicels 1·5-2·5 cm. long. *Calyx-tube* 1·2 cm. long; lobes spreading, lanceolate, a little shorter than the tube, keeled. *Corolla-tube* about 2 cm. long, narrowly subcylindric, more or less curved, glabrous or minutely puberulous;

lobes 1·5 cm. long, 0·8 cm. broad, obovate, rounded, the upper 2 connate high up. *Stamens* 4, in 2 pairs; filaments clothed with long hairs, the upper pair shorter than the lower pair; anthers 1-celled, oblong, dorsifixed. *Ovary* oblong-ovoid; style terete; stigma thickened. *Capsule* 1·2 cm. long, 8 mm. in diameter, obliquely ovoid, obliquely beaked at the apex, glabrous.

PLATE 50.—Fig. 1, plant, natural size; Fig. 2, corolla, front view; Fig. 3, corolla, back view; Fig. 4, stamens; Fig. 5, corolla laid open; Fig. 6, gynaecium; Fig. 7, cross-section of ovary; Fig. 8, calyx; Fig. 9, capsule. All enlarged except Fig. 1.

F.P.S.A., 1922.

S. GOWER DEL.

PLATE 51.

GAZANIA SUBULATA.
Cape Province.

COMPOSITAE. TRIBE ARCTOTIDEAE.

GAZANIA, Gaertn.; Benth. et Hook. f. Gen. Plant.
Gazania subulata, *R. Br. in Ait. Hort. Kew. ed. II. vol. v. p. 140; Fl.*

The native species of *Gazania* receive perhaps more attention from gardeners than other groups of South African *Compositae*. This is due to their easy cultivation and the brightness of their "flowers." The general names "Gousblom" and "Marigolds" are applied indiscriminately to various species of *Gazania*, *Arctotis* and *Dimorphotheca*.

Our plate was prepared from plants flowering at the Division of Botany, Pretoria. The plant is acquiescent and forms a compact clump about 2 feet in diameter. It flowers freely and is easily propagated. We hope in future numbers to illustrate all the better known kinds of "Gousblom," especially some of the beautiful Namaqualand species.

Our specimen bears out Harvey's statement that this species and *G. longiscapa* are scarcely distinct, as it agrees with *G. subulata* in having the peduncle pilose and with *G. longiscapa* in the cartilaginous-ciliate leaves which are glabrous on the mid-rib below.

Specimens of the plant figured are preserved in the National Herbarium, Pretoria (Herb. No. 1447).

DESCRIPTION:—An acaulescent plant. *Leaves* radical, crowded,

10-40 cm. long, 2-6 mm. broad, linear, subacute, with a short spine at the apex, narrowed and channelled below and sheathing at the base, dark green and glabrous above, white tomentose beneath, except on the midrib, with the margins spinulose-ciliate. *Peduncle* 24 cm. long, terete, hollow, pilose on the uppermost third, with 1 or 2 bracts. *Involucral scales* connate at the base; tube 1 cm. long, 7 mm. in diameter, glabrous, intruse at the base; scales in three rows, 1-1·5 cm. long; the outer linear-acuminate, acute, with spinulose margins; the inner ovate, acuminate, acute, with membranous margins. *Receptacle* convex, honeycombed. *Ray-florets* neuter, 3·2 cm. long; the limb 1·2 cm. broad, obovate-oblong, obtuse, with a broad mouse-coloured band beneath and about 15-veined. *Disc florets* hermaphrodite, 1-2 cm. long; tube 5-angled; lobes 4 mm. long, linear-oblong, obtuse. *Anthers* minutely tailed at the base. *Pappus* of delicate linear acuminate scales hidden by the long hairs which cover the ovary. *Ovary* densely villous; style with a thickened ring about the middle; lobes linear, obtuse.

PLATE 51.—Fig. 1, flowers and leaves; Fig. 2, upper portion of style; Fig. 3, stamens; Fig. 4, longitudinal section of capitulum with hairs from ovary removed; Fig. 5, corolla laid open; Fig. 6, disc-floret, showing pappus, with hairs from the ovary removed; Fig. 7, plant, much reduced.

F.P.S.A., 1922.

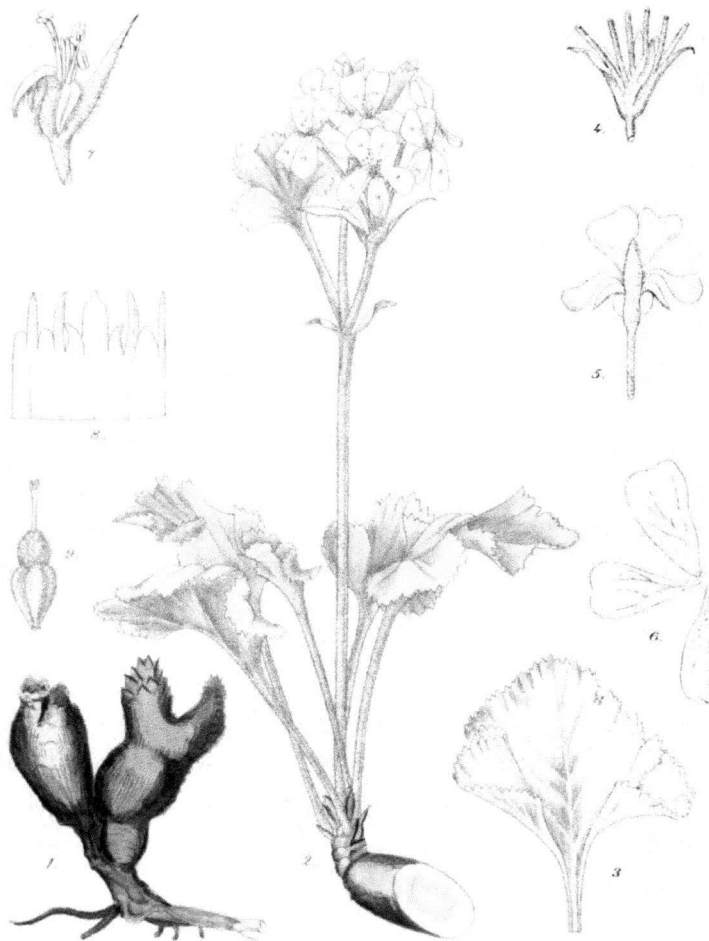

S. GOWER DEL.

PLATE 52.

PELARGONIUM CRASSICAULE.
South-West Africa.

GERANIACEAE. TRIBE PELARGONIEAE.

PELARGONIUM, L'Her.; Benth. et Hook. f. Gen. Plant.
Pelargonium crassicaule, *L'Her. Ger. t. 36; Fl.*

This species of *Pelargonium* is one of the many botanical curiosities found in the arid regions of South-West Africa, where the native plants have to contend against very adverse conditions. In the dry season the plant loses its leaves and assumes a knobby appearance due to the thick rather woody stems. The leaves appear after the rains and are more or less crowded at the ends of the branches.

The species was first discovered by Mr. Ant. Hove in 1786 in South-West Africa, and was introduced by him into Kew Gardens the same year. In 1799 a figure was published in the *Botanical Magazine* (t. 477) prepared from a plant which flowered with Messrs. Grimwood & Co., Kensington, London. Though this figure does not quite agree with our specimen in the markings of the petals, we have no doubt that it represents the plant here illustrated, which can only be considered as a variety.

Our plant was collected by Dr. I. B. Pole Evans, C.M.G., who states that it is common on rocky outcrops in the Nabib Desert at Luderitzbuch. It has been established and flowered at the Gardens of the Division of Botany, Pretoria. Specimens are preserved in the National Herbarium, Pretoria (Herb. No. 1452).

DESCRIPTION:—*Stems* woody and swollen, with blackish bark. *Leaves* crowded at the apex of the branches; petioles 4-11 cm. long, semiterete, finely pilose with reflexed hairs; lamina 2-5 cm. long, 2-4·5 cm. broad, rounded-ovate, slightly 3-lobed, rounded above, cuneate at the base and merging into the petiole, with crinkled bluntly dentate margins and prominent veins beneath, finely pilose above and below; stipules brown, 4 mm. long, acuminate from an ovate base. *Peduncle* 7·5 cm. long, terete, finely pilose with reflexed hairs, branching above. *Involucral bracts* 1·2 cm. long, lanceolate, acute, pilose. *Umbel* 6-flowered; pedicels about 1-2 cm. long. *Flowers* faintly sweet scented. *Petals* 1·25 cm. long, 6 mm. broad, obovate, rounded or truncate at the apex; the three lower produced into a linear claw 2 mm. long; the two upper slightly connate. *Calyx-tube* 2 mm. long, terete, pilose; sepals all pilose; upper sepal erect, 8 mm. long, 2·5 mm. broad, ovate-lanceolate, obtuse; lower and lateral sepals reflexed, 8 mm. long, 1·5-2 mm. broad, lanceolate, obtuse. *Stamens* 7, in three rows of 2, 3 and 2; filaments linear, 4·7 mm. long, connate at the base; anthers 1·75 mm. long, oblong; staminodes 3, shorter than the filaments. Ovary 1·5 mm. long, densely pilose above; styles united for 1·5 mm. and then separating into 6 stigmas 1·5 mm. long.

PLATE 52.—Fig. 1, plant as it appears in dry seasons; Fig. 2, plant with leaves and flowers; Fig. 3, lamina of leaf; Fig. 4, involucre at base of flowers; Fig. 5, back view of flower; Fig. 6, petals; Fig. 7, calyx with stamens; Fig. 8, filaments and staminodes; Fig. 9, gynaecium.

F.P.S.A., 1922.

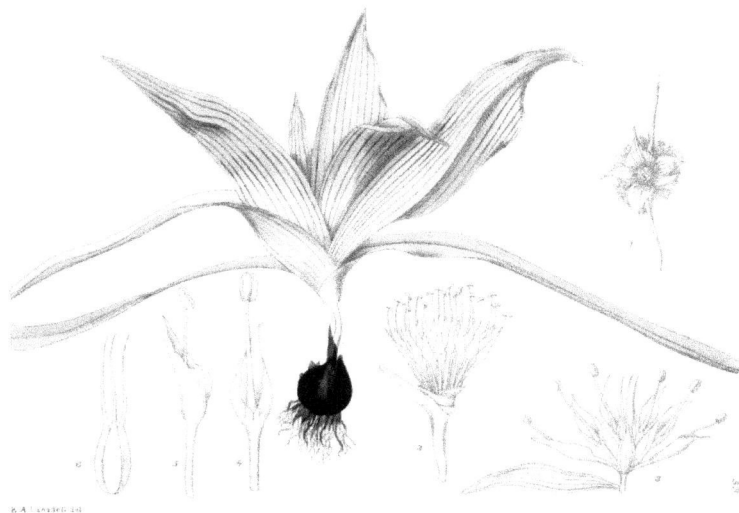

K. A. LANSDELL DEL.

PLATE 53.

ANDROCYMBIUM MELANTHIOIDES.

Cape Province, Natal, Transvaal.

LILIACEAE. TRIBE ANGUILLARIEAE.

ANDROCYMBIUM, Willd.; Benth. et Hook. f. Gen. Plant.
Androcymbium melanthioides, *Willd. in Ges.*
Naturf. fr. Berl. Mag. vol. ii. p. 21; Fl.

The genus *Androcymbium* is represented by about eighteen species, two of which are known from the Mediterranean Region and two from Tropical Africa, the remainder of the species being confined to South Africa.

Our plate was prepared from specimens collected by Dr. I. B. Pole Evans at Silverton, near Pretoria, in May, 1921, and represents the best known and most widely distributed species of the genus. The plant shows the characteristic habit of all the species, viz. stemless, with the flower head hidden by large bracts which may be white, green, or purplish. In cultivation it does not lend itself to planting out, but makes a striking and pleasing object when placed singly in pots.

Specimens of the plant figured are preserved in the National Herbarium, Pretoria (Herb. No. 1451).

DESCRIPTION:—A stemless plant. *Bulb* about 1·5 cm. in diameter, globose, covered with more or less hardened black tunics. *Leaves* 2-3, 14-22 cm. long, linear from an ovate base, acutely acuminate, glabrous. *Bracts* white or purplish, several,

3-8·5 cm. long, ·8-3·5 cm. broad, oblong, ovate-oblong or ovate, obtuse or sometimes apiculate at the apex, sometimes acuminate, many nerved (up to 50-nerved). *Head* about 6-flowered, hidden and overtopped by the bracts. *Bracts* subtending the flowers about 3·5 cm. long, lanceolate, acute, 5-nerved. *Pedicel* 3 mm. long, 2·5 mm. broad above, obovoid, fleshy. *Perianth segments* produced into a distinct claw; claw 5 mm. long, 1 mm. broad, with a more or less distinct keel; blade 6 mm. long, 3 mm. broad, ovate, cucullate, acuminate, 3-keeled. *Stamens* inserted at the junction of the claw and blade; filaments 9 mm. long, terete; anthers 3 mm. long, elliptic. *Ovary* 6 mm. long, 2·5 mm. in diameter, ellipsoid, subtrigonous; styles free, 8 mm. long, terete; stigma simple,

---

PLATE 53.—Fig. 1, plant viewed from above (reduced); Fig. 2, inflorescence; Fig. 3, flower with bract; Fig. 4, perianth segment with stamen, front view; Fig. 5, perianth segment with stamen, side view; Fig. 6, gynaecium.

F.P.S.A., 1922.

S. Gower del.

S. GOWER DEL.

PLATE 54.

MESEMBRYANTHEMUM ALOIDES.
Bechuanaland.

FICOIDEAE. TRIBE MEBEMBRYANTHEMEAE.

MESEMBRYANTHEMUM, Linn.; Benth. et Hook. f.
Mesembryanthemum aloides, *Haw. Suppl. p. 88; Fl.*

This extremely rare plant, which was first found by Burchell at Metlowing and at Jabirn Fontein, near Takun in Bechuanaland, in 1812, was recently rediscovered by Dr. I. B. Pole Evans near Postmas Berg, and has been established in the garden of the Division of Botany, Pretoria. In the *Journal of the Linnean Society* (vol. xlv. p. 123) for 1920, Mr. N. E. Brown gives a fuller description of the species based mainly on a coloured drawing of the plant made by Burchell, who states that the roots are "eaten by natives as a substitute for better food."

The specimen from which the present plate was prepared flowered at Pretoria in August, and has enabled us to draw up a more complete description.

Specimens are preserved in the National Herbarium.

DESCRIPTION:—A stemless plant. *Root* thick and woody. *Leaves* tufted, 8-12 in a cluster, forming a rosette about 9 cm. in diameter, 3-5.5 cm. long, 1-1.7 cm. broad in the widest part, lanceolate-spathulate viewed from above, acuminate, obtuse, mucronate at the apex and shaped like the bow of a boat, slightly narrowed at the base and sheathing, flat above, keeled beneath, dotted with white spots on both surfaces. *Flowers* lemon-yellow, sessile between the leaves. *Calyx-tube* 2·2 cm. long, widening from a cylindrical base to 1·2 cm. in diameter above, sparsely pustulate above; lobes of two different lengths, pustulate; the longer 1·7 cm. long, ovate, acuminate; the shorter 9 mm. long with membranous margins. *Corolla* 2·5 cm. in diameter when expanded; petals up to 1 cm. long, 1 mm. broad, linear, obtuse. *Filaments* about 5 mm. long, hairy at the base. *Ovary* 10-celled; styles 10 free. *Fruit* not seen.

PLATE 54.—Fig. 1, calyx and calyx lobes; Fig. 2, petal; Fig. 3, stamen; Fig. 4, top of ovary showing styles; Fig. 5, transverse section of ovary; Fig. 6, longitudinal section of leaf; Fig. 7, transverse section of leaf near the apex; Fig. 8, apex of leaf.

F.P.S.A., 1922.

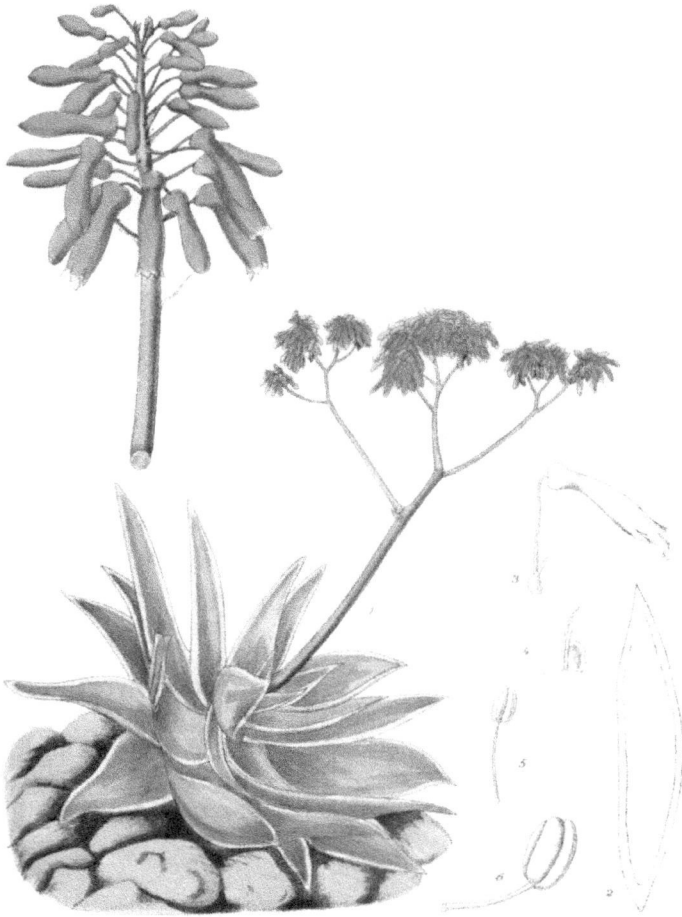

K. A. LANSDELL DEL.

PLATE 55.

ALOE STRIATA.
Cape Province.

LILIACEAE. TRIBE ALOINEAE.

ALOE, Linn.; Benth. et Hook. f. Gen. Plant.
Aloe striata, *Haw. in Trans. Linn. Soc.*

This is the well-known "Coral Aloe" of South Africa. It is typical of both the Upper and Lower Karroo regions and also of the Namaqualand region. The species is generally found on dry rocky slopes, and the plants assume a subdecumbent position, very rarely growing erect. It is the only South African species of *Aloe* which bears leaves without prickly teeth. In the dry summer season the leaves lose their bluish-grey colour and become a copper-red, which gives the plants a very characteristic appearance in the veld. A large number of hybrids have been raised by crossing this species with others belonging to the *Saponaria* group, and a hybrid, described as *Aloe Lynchii*, was obtained between this and *Gasteria verrucosa*.

The late Prof. MacOwan states that sun-birds (*Nectarineae*) are the pollinating agents of *Aloe striata* and some other species of *Aloe*, and if the birds are kept away by covering the inflorescence with wire netting, few or no capsules are produced.

Our specimen was collected by Dr. I. B. Pole Evans at Dassie Deur near Port Elizabeth, and flowered in the garden of the Division of Botany, Pretoria, in August.

Specimens are preserved in the National Herbarium.

DESCRIPTION:—*Stem* underground. *Leaves* about 13, crowded in a basal rosette, up to 30 cm. long, 6-11·5 cm. broad, oblong, oblong-lanceolate, or the inner ovate, acuminate, flat, bluish-grey, glaucous, faintly many-nerved, with pink margins. *Peduncle* about 24 cm. long, branched above; at the base flat on one side, convex on the other; in the upper portion semiterete. *Inflorescence* a panicle of racemes, the ultimate racemes 6-9 cm. long, lax. *Bracts* subtending the racemes about 1 cm. long, membranous, ovate, acuminate. *Floral bracts* 3 mm. long, ovate, acuminate, acute, membranous. *Pedicels* about 1 cm. long, spreading. *Flowers* more or less pendulous. *Perianth-tube* in mature flowers 2 cm. long, globose at the base, then slightly constricted, then gradually widening into a tube 6 mm. in diameter at the throat; lobes about 3 mm. long, ovate, rounded at the apex. *Stamens* included or slightly exserted; filaments attached at the base of the perianth-tube, 1·7 cm. long; anthers about 1 mm. long. *Ovary* 5 mm. long, oblong; style 1·7 cm. long, terete; stigma faintly 3-lobed. *Immature fruit* 2 cm. long, 1·1 cm. in diameter, ellipsoid, subtrigonous.

PLATE 55.—Fig. 1, plant showing characteristic habit; Fig. 2, transverse section of leaf; Fig. 3, flower; Fig. 4, bract; Fig. 5, stamen; Fig. 6, young fruit.

F.P.S.A., 1922.

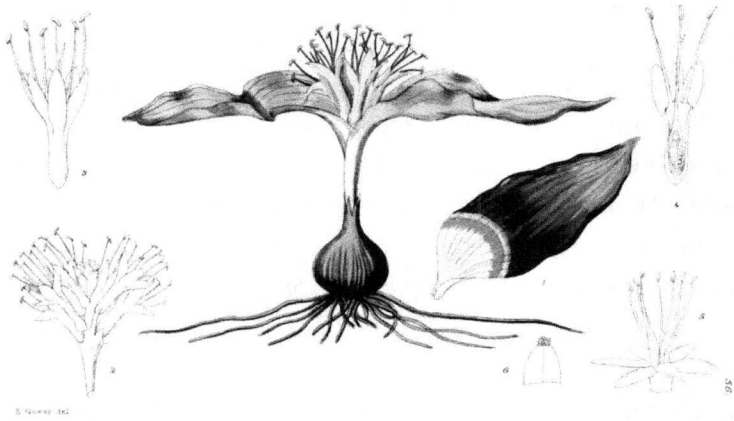

S. GOWER DEL.

PLATE 56.

LILIACEAE. TRIBE SCILLEAE.

POLYXENA, Kunth.; Benth. et Hook. Gen. Plant.
Polyxena haemanthoides, *Baker in Hook. Ic. t. 1727; Fl.*

This rare species was recently collected by Dr. Marloth in the Calvinia Division, and to our knowledge has not been collected since the late Dr. Bolus discovered it on the Nieuwveld Mountains near Fraserburg over thirty years ago. *Polyxena* is a small endemic genus of about a dozen species, the majority of which are very little known, as most of them have not been collected since they were first found by the early Cape botanical collectors. Baker, who described and figured this species in Hooker's *Icones*, remarks, "The affinity of this interesting novelty is evidently close with *Massonia rugulosa* of Lichtenstein and *M. marginata* of Willdenow, of neither of which we possess specimens in the Kew Herbarium." Both of them fall under the genus *Polyxena*, as defined in the *Genera Plantarum*. Specimens preserved in the National Herbarium, Pretoria (Herb. No. 1448).

DESCRIPTION:—*Bulb* about 3-4 cm. in diameter, ovoid. *Leaves* two, lying flat on the ground, 7 cm. long, 2·5-3 cm. broad, lanceolate or ovate-lanceolate, acute, narrowing at the base, glabrous, about 10-nerved, with scabrous margins. *Inflorescence* a contracted raceme, about 12-flowered. *Bracts* white, 5 mm. long, ovate, acuminate. *Flowers* sessile; perianth-tube 1·3 cm. long, 3·5 mm.

in diameter, slightly compressed; lobes in 2 rows, 9 mm. long, 3 mm. broad, lanceolate-oblong, obtuse, glandular at the apex. *Stamens* in a single row; filaments united into a tube at the base, 1·5 cm. long; anthers 3 mm. long, linear, versatile. *Ovary* 6 mm. long, oblong in outline; style 1·5 cm. long, terete; stigma simple.

PLATE 56.—Fig. 1, leaf; Fig. 2, inflorescence showing coma; Fig. 3, flower; Fig. 4, flower in longitudinal section; Fig. 5, upper portion of perianth showing stamens and style; Fig. 6, apex of perianth lobe.

F.P.S.A., 1922.

57

K. A. LANSDELL DEL.

PLATE 57.

DIMORPHOTHECA SPECTABILIS.

Transvaal.

COMPOSITAE. TRIBE CALENDULACEAE.

DIMORPHOTHECA, Moench.; Benth. et Hook. f. Gen. Plant.
Dimorphotheca spectabilis, *Schltr. in Journ. Bot.*

For quite a considerable time this common and well-known *Dimorphotheca* was placed in herbaria under the name of *Dimorphotheca Ecklonis*, and Harvey, who examined specimens of this plant collected by Burke and Zeyher on the Aapies River and Magaliesberg, also included it under *D. Ecklonis*. Dr. Schlechter first recognised that the Transvaal plant was an undescribed species, but apparently did not realise that Burke and Zeyher had collected the plant close on a hundred years ago, as he founded his description on specimens collected by Mr. E. E. Galpin, F.L.S., in 1887, on the Saddleback Mountains, Barberton.

Dimorphotheca spectabilis is a spring flowering plant, and is common around Pretoria during the months of September and October. It is a well-grown plant with large mauve flowers, and if introduced into cultivation would be an acquisition to any garden. The plant sets seed freely, and could easily be raised by this means. The species is poisonous, and in experiments carried out by the Division of Veterinary Research, the plant was found to cause death in sheep fed on it.

Specimens are preserved in the National Herbarium, Pretoria (Herb. No. 1470).

DESCRIPTION:—An herbaceous plant 24-40 cm. high with one or more stems arising from the apex of a stout deep underground root. *Stem* terete, faintly furrowed, covered with short glandular hairs. *Leaves* 2-4 cm. long, ·6-1 cm. broad, lanceolate or lanceolate-ovate, obtuse, tapering upwards from a broad base, sometimes slightly narrowed at the base, with a prominent midrib and two faint lateral nerves more distinct on the upper surface, punctate-glandular on both surfaces, and with glandular hairs beneath, ciliate with glandular hairs. *Flower head* solitary at the ends of the stems. *Peduncle* 6-10 cm. long, terete, furrowed, glandular-pubescent. *Involucral-scales* in 2 rows, somewhat connate at the base, 1·3-2 cm. long, ovate, acuminate, acute with membranous margins, glandular-pubescent. *Receptacle* 7 mm. broad, convex, hollow. *Ray florets* female. *Corolla-tube* 2 mm. long, cylindric, glandular-pilose; limb 2 cm. long, 4 mm. broad, linear, 3-toothed at the apex, glandular-pilose on the back at the base. *Style* as long as the corolla-tube. *Disc florets* hermaphrodite. *Corolla-tube* 5 mm. long, cylindric, constricted and narrower near the base, sparsely covered with glandular hairs on the broader portion of the tube; lobes 2 mm. long, almost 1 mm. broad, lanceolate, obtuse. *Filaments* 4 mm. long, linear; anthers 3·5 mm. long, with deep golden-yellow pollen. *Pappus* none. *Ovary* 3 mm. long, flattened, winged and 2-horned at the apex; style 6 mm. long, cylindric; lobes 1 mm. long, truncate at the apex. *Fruit* 1·5 cm. long, flattened, orbicular, with a circular wing.

PLATE 57.—Fig. 1, whole plant showing habit (reduced); Fig. 2, flower bud; Fig. 3, disk flower; Fig. 4, ray flower with ovary removed.

F.P.S.A., 1922.

K. A. LANSDELL DEL.

PLATE 58.

MIMETES CAPITULATA.
Cape Province.

PROTEACEAE. TRIBE PROTEAE.

MIMETES, Salisb.; Benth. et Hook. f. Gen. Plant.
Mimetes capitulata, *R. Br. in Trans. Linn. Soc.*

The genus *Mimetes* constitutes a small group of South African Proteaceae of nine species, all confined to the South-Western area of the Cape Province. The genus was first founded by Salisbury, but for over one hundred years afterwards plants belonging to two other distinct genera were placed under the name *Mimetes*. One of these, *Orothamnus Zeyheri*, we figured on Plate 38 of this work. Like a great many other groups of South African plants the species of *Mimetes* have not been extensively collected, and we are indebted to Mr. T. P. Stokoe, of Cape Town, who has rediscovered so many interesting plants on the Hottentot Hollands Mountains, for the opportunity of figuring the present species. The examination of the fresh material has enabled us to add a few descriptive details to the description given in the *Flora Capensis*.

Specimens are preserved in the National Herbarium, Pretoria (Herb. No. 1457).

DESCRIPTION:—*Branches* villous. *Leaves* 1·2-3 cm. long, ·5-1·5 cm. broad, lanceolate, lanceolate-ovate or ovate, gradually narrowed to an obtuse callous apex, a little narrowed at the base, entire, coriaceous, indistinctly 3-nerved, densely adpressed-villous with silky hairs. *Heads* sessile, 2·5-3·3 cm. long, 10-16 flowered, in the axils of the leaves at the ends of the branches. *Involucral-bracts* 5-6-seriate, varying from linear-lanceolate to ovate-lanceolate, more or less narrowed at the base, membranous, pubescent outside, long-ciliate. *Receptacle* long-setose. *Perianth-segments* free or nearly so, 2·5-3 cm. long, linear-filiform, slightly widened for about 5 mm. at the base, plumose, limb about 4 mm. long, linear-lanceolate, subacute, long-villous on the back. *Anthers* subsessile, about 2 mm. long, linear, with a lanceolate, subacute, concave apical gland. *Hypogynous scales* 1 mm. long, linear, obtuse, white. *Ovary* 2 mm. long, oblong in outline, pubescent; style 4 cm. long, subcylindric above, furrowed on the lower half and usually twisted at the junction with the ovary, swollen with an ellipsoid portion below the stigma, glabrous; stigma about 4 mm. long, furrowed, with an oblique ovoid acuminate subacute apex and with a distinct collar at the base.

PLATE 58.—Fig. 1, capitulum; Fig. 2, a single flower showing portion of hairy receptacle; Fig. 3, perianth segment; Fig. 4, pistil.

F.P.S.A., 1922.

K. A. LANSDELL DEL.

PLATE 59.

ERYTHRINA CAFFRA.
Cape Province, Natal, Transvaal.

LEGUMINOSAE. TRIBE PHASEOLEAE.

ERYTHRINA, Linn.; Benth. et Hook. f. Gen. Plant.
Erythrina caffra, *Thunb. Fl.*

This species is a common tree in the eastern parts of the Cape Province and also in the coastal and midland districts of Natal. The plant is known as the "Kaffir Boom," and to children in Natal as "Cookie Doodles." The Zulu name for the tree is "Umsini."

The wood is very soft, and the only use to which it is put is for fencing poles, as it easily takes root and is free from the attack of termites. The scarlet seeds are strung as necklaces.

In various parts of the country the tree may be seen in cultivation, and when in full bloom the bright scarlet flowers make it extremely ornamental. The tree is deciduous and the flowers appear in spring while the plant is still leafless, but occasionally leaves and flowers may be produced at the same time.

Our plate was prepared from material collected by Miss K. A. Lansdell on the Berea, Durban, Natal. Specimens are preserved in the National Herbarium, Pretoria (Herb. No. 1456).

DESCRIPTION:—A tree 6-17 m. high. *Branches* pale-coloured, rugose, prickly, the prickles dark-coloured, up to 7 mm. or more long, broad at the base, usually a little curved, very sharp. *Leaves* clustered near the ends of the twigs, trifoliolate: common petiole up to 21 cm. long, unarmed; terminal leaflet 6·5-9 cm. long, 9-11·5 cm. broad, ovate or sometimes sub 3-lobed, usually acuminate, more or less cuneate at the base, glabrous with two small glands at the base of the petiolule; lateral leaflets 6·5-9 cm. long, 6·5-9 cm. broad, similar in shape to the terminal leaflet, usually acuminate, glabrous. *Inflorescence* a many-flowered dense raceme, 4·6 cm. long; flowers pendulous: peduncle dark brown, 7·5-15 cm. long, terete, velvety. *Calyx* up to 1 cm. long, more or less tubular campanulate, 2-lipped, velvety-brown outside. *Vexillum* up to 5 cm. long, 2·5 cm. broad when expanded, conduplicate, falcate; alae yellow-green, 4-8 mm. long, oblong, curved; carina equalling the alae. *Stamens* 10, exserted; the vexillary filament free to the base. *Ovary* stalked, villous; stigma simple. *Legume* few-seeded, constricted between the seeds. *Seeds* scarlet, with a black hilum.

PLATE 59.—Fig. 1, vexillum; Fig. 2, carina; Fig. 3, wing; Fig. 4, calyx; Fig. 5, stamens; Fig. 6, gynaecium; Fig. 7, fruit, showing one seed.

F.P.S.A., 1922.

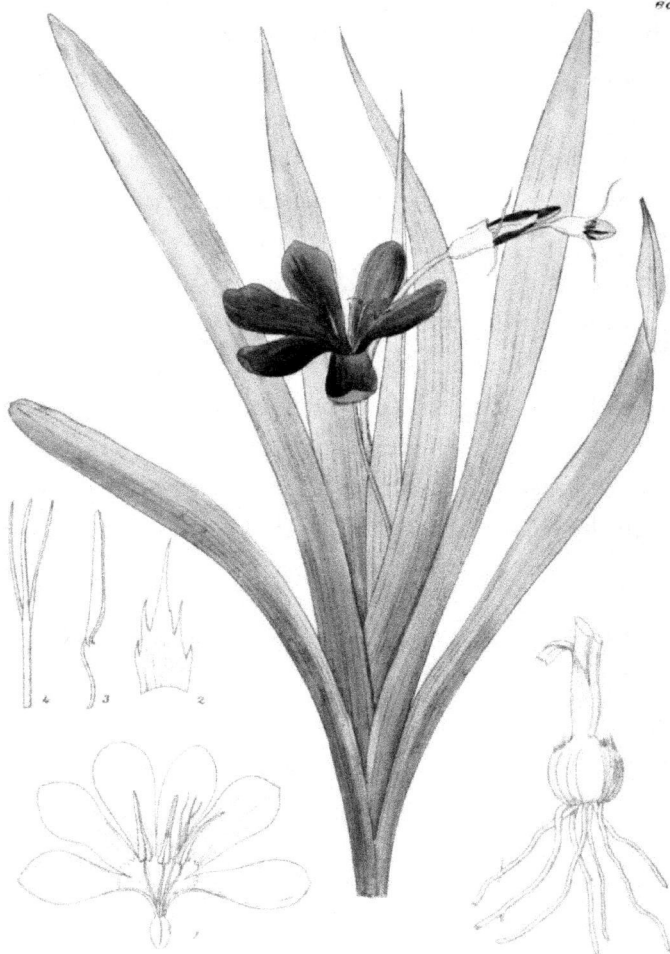

K. A. LANSDELL DEL.

PLATE 60.

SPARAXIS GRANDIFLORA.
Cape Province.

IRIDACEAE. TRIBE IXIEAE.

SPARAXIS, Ker; Benth. et Hook. f. Gen. Plant.
Sparaxis grandiflora, *Ker in Konig and Sims' Ann. i. 225; Fl.*

The plant here figured was introduced into Kew Gardens in the year 1758. Though it has been more than once illustrated in botanical publications, we do not apologise for reproducing this coloured illustration of one of the common bulbs found in so many gardens at the Cape. The species *grandiflora* is represented by many colour varieties, and is probably the same as the plant described as *Spiraxis tricolor*, which only appears to differ from it in the colour markings on the perianth. The variety here figured is probably the form originally described under the name *Spiraxis atropurpurea*.

The specimens were collected by Dr. R. Marloth, who forwarded them to the Division of Botany, Pretoria, where they flowered in August. They are preserved in the National Herbarium (Herb. No. 1454).

DESCRIPTION:—*Bulb* 1·3 cm. long, 1·3 cm. in diameter, covered with light-coloured fibrous tunics. *Leaves* about 10 to a bulb, distichous; the lower leaves about 5 cm. long and 4 mm. broad; the upper up to 26 cm. long and 1·2 cm. broad; all linear, acuminate, acute, with a distinct midrib and the inner margin membranous, sheathing at the base, glabrous. *Inflorescence* shorter than the upper leaves; peduncle about 12 cm. long, clasped and hidden by the inner leaves. *Flowers* about 6 to an inflorescence, purple. *Bracts* membranous, 1 cm. long, awned or lacerated with the awns up to 1·2 cm. long. *Perianth-tube* 9 mm. long, cylindric in the lower half, campanulate in the upper half; lobes 1·5 cm. long, 7 mm. broad, spathulate-obovate. *Stamens* attached to the throat of the perianth-tube; filaments 9 mm. long; anthers 1·3 cm. long, linear, eared at the base. *Ovary* 4 mm. long, 2·5 mm. in diameter, oblong; style 1·5 cm. long, terete; stigmas 8 mm. long.

PLATE 60.—Fig. 1, perianth laid open; Fig. 2, bract; Fig. 3, stamen; Fig. 4, style and stigmas.

F.P.S.A., 1922.

61

K. A. LANSDELL DEL.

PLATE 61.

CORYCIUM CRISPUM.
Cape Province, Little Namaqualand.

ORCHIDACEAE. TRIBE OPHRYDEAE.

CORYCIUM, Sw.; Benth. et Hook. f. Gen. Plant.
Corycium crispum, *Sw. in Vet. Acad. Handl. Stockh.,*
1800, 222; Bolus, Orchids of South Africa, vol. i. t. 45; Fl.

This extremely pretty little orchid was sent to us by Mrs. E. Rood from Van Rhynsdorp in August. Though the late Dr. Bolus published a figure of this species in his "Orchids of South Africa," we again reproduce a plate of the plant, and it is the first member of the family *Orchidaceae* to appear in this work. The species is fairly common in the Cape Province extending from the Cape Peninsula up to Clanwilliam and Van Rhynsdorp and into Little Namaqualand. It has been known to botanical science for a considerable time, and was first described under its present name over 100 years ago.

The species belongs to the large group of terrestrial orchids which are characteristic of the south-western region of the Cape Province, the few epiphytic orchids which are found in South Africa being mostly confined to the forest regions of the Eastern Province and the Northern Transvaal.

Specimens are preserved in the National Herbarium, Pretoria (Herb. No. 1467).

DESCRIPTION:—*Plant* up to 18 cm. high. *Tuber* 3 cm. long, 1·5 cm. in diameter, egg-shaped. *Leaves* cauline, somewhat spreading and imbricate, 8-10 cm. long, 2·5 cm. broad, linear-lanceolate to ovate, very acuminate, with undulate margins. *Inflorescence* 9-10 cm. long, many-flowered. *Bracts* 2 cm. long, 1·7 cm. broad, ovate, shortly acuminate, as long as the ovary. *Flowers* sessile. *Dorsal sepal* 8 mm. long, linear; lateral sepals connate into a bilobed limb, erect in young flowers, becoming deflexed in older flowers. *Side petals* 8 mm. long, 6 mm. broad above, deeply concave and saccate at the base; lip adnate to the column, horizontal, with a limb 5 mm. broad from a distinct claw. *Arms of rostellum* rounded, recurved and projecting into the concavity of the side petals.

PLATE 61.—Fig. 1, bract; Fig. 2, petal; Fig. 3, dorsal sepal; Fig. 4, lip; Fig. 5, ovary; Fig. 6, column showing anthers; Fig. 7, column showing stigmas; Fig. 8, side view of column.

F.P.S.A., 1922.

K. A. LANSDELL DEL.

PLATE 62.

ALOE EXCELSA.
Rhodesia.

LILIACEAE. TRIBE ALOINEAE.

ALOE, Linn.; Benth. et Hook. f. Gen. Plant.
Aloe excelsa, *Berger in Notizblatt. Berl. Bot. Gart. u.*
Museums, vol. iv. (1906) 247; Das Pflanzenreich.

This arborescent Aloe forms one of the most conspicuous features of the vegetation of the Matoppos in Rhodesia in July and August, when it brightens up the Kopjes with its crimson flowers. Full-grown plants vary in height from 15-20 feet, and one of their chief characteristics is the graceful recurving of the ends of the leaves. Our illustration is made from one of the many plants of this species which adorn the rockeries of the Union Buildings, and which were collected by Mr. J. Wickens on the Matoppos. The plants thrive well in Pretoria, and attract consideration through their deep carmine inflorescence. They flower in Pretoria during August and September.

Specimens are preserved in the National Herbarium (Herb. No. 1453).

DESCRIPTION:—Aborescent up to 5-6·3 m. high. *Stems* about 3-4 cm. in diameter. *Leaves* crowded and forming a rosette at the end of the stem up to 0·2 m. long, 8-9 cm. broad at the base, gradually narrowing to the apex, lanceolate-ovate, acuminate, with the uppermost third gracefully recurved, deeply channelled above, convex beneath, with spines along the margin and with spines on the under surface; spines 4 mm. long, 5 mm. apart below and about 2·6 cm. apart on the upper portion of the leaf. *Inflorescence* a panicle; peduncle 13-16 cm. long, compressed, convex on both surfaces, with a prominent ridge on either side. *Bracts* ovate, acute, membranous. *Ultimate racemes* 22-25 cm. long, 5·5 cm. in diameter, cylindric, densely many-flowered. *Floral-bracts* brown, about 5 mm. long, 5 mm. broad at the base, ovate, acute. *Flowers* subsessile; perianth-tube 1 cm. long, 5 mm. in diameter, oblong in outline; lobes 1·8 cm. long, 0·6 mm. broad, oblong, obtuse, 3-nerved, the outer with a small rostrate body just below the apex; the inner perianth-segments free to the base. *Ovary* 5 mm. long, 3 mm. broad, oblong; style 2·7 cm. long, cylindric; stigma simple.

PLATE 62.—Fig. 1, plant much reduced; Fig. 2, stamens; Fig. 3, perianth-segments; Fig. 4, apices of outer and inner perianth-segments; Fig. 5, flower; Fig. 6, bract; Fig. 7, leaf; Fig. 8, transverse section of leaf.

F.P.S.A., 1922.

K. A. LANSDELL DEL.

PLATE 63.

GLADIOLUS ALATUS, var. NAMAQUENSIS.
Cape Province.

IRIDACEAE. TRIBE IXIEAE.

GLADIOLUS, Linn.; Benth. et Hook. f. Gen. Plant.
Gladiolus alatus, var. namaquensis, *Baker in Fl.*

This plant is a variety of the Cape "Kalkoentje" (*Gladiolus alatus*), and might conveniently be called the "Namaqua Kalkoentje." This particular variety has been known for almost 200 years, and in the Banksian Herbarium in the British Museum is a well-preserved specimen which was collected by Masson in Namaqualand. A figure of the plant prepared from specimens which flowered in England was published in the *Botanical Magazine* in 1801.

In the veld groups of plants are usually found together, each forming a corm which has developed as an offshoot from the parent corm. This character would render the plant easy of propagation.

We are indebted to Mrs. E. Rood of van Rhynsdorp for specimens which were received by the Division of Botany in September, 1921. They are preserved in the National Herbarium, Pretoria (Herb. No. 1468).

DESCRIPTION:—*Corm* covered with fibrous tunics. *Stem* with a basal sheath 2·5-3·5 cm. long. *Leaves* four, decreasing in size upwards; the outermost leaf 13-15 cm. long, 2·5-3 cm. broad; upper leaves 7-12 cm. long, ·5-2·1 cm. broad, all lanceolate, acuminate, clasping and equitant at the base, 5-nerved, with reddish margins; the innermost almost wholly clasping. *Visible peduncle* about 11 cm. long, 3-flowered. *Outer-bracts* 4 cm. long, 2 cm. broad, boat-shaped, acuminate, sharply keeled, with keel and margins reddish-brown; inner similar to the outer but bifid at the apex. *Perianth-tube* 1 cm. long, cylindric below, campanulate above; upper segments 2·5 cm. long, 2·2 cm. broad, ovate, subacuminate; 2 lower segments 2 cm. long, 5 mm. broad above, obovate, narrowed into a long linear claw; the lowermost segment 1·1 cm. broad, ovate, subacuminate. *Filaments* 1·5 cm. long, cylindric; anthers 1·3 cm. long, linear. *Ovary* 8 mm. long, 2·5 mm. in diameter, narrowly ellipsoid; style 3 cm. long, filiform; lobes 5 mm. long, linear, slightly broadened above, rounded and bifid at the apex.

PLATE 63.—Fig. 1, corm; Fig. 2, lower perianth-segment; Fig. 3, lateral perianth segment; Fig. 4, stamens, front and side view; Fig. 5, style and stigmas.

F.P.S.A., 1922.

S. GOWER DEL.

PLATE 64.

COMPOSITAE. TRIBE ARCTOTIDEAE.

GAZANIA, Gaertn.; Benth. et Hook. f. Gen. Plant.
Gazania pygmaea, *Sond. in Linnaea.*

During the month of September the veld round Pretoria is carpeted with the white flowers of this little *Gazania*. It is one of the first, if not the first plant to flower on burnt veld, and the contrast in colour between the white flowers and the young green grass is very striking. While so extremely common during the spring months, this species appears to be little known botanically. It was evidently first collected by the botanist Karl Zeyher on the Magaliesberg about the year 1841, and the description in the *Flora Capensis* based on Zeyher's specimen is the most recent published information we have about this species. The plants are tufted, several underground stems arising from a stout tap-root.

The present plate was prepared from specimens collected by Mr. D. Fouche on the outskirts of Pretoria. Specimens are preserved in the National Herbarium, Pretoria.

DESCRIPTION:—Acaulescent plants with several subterranean stems from the apex of the deep tap-root. *Leaves* crowded, radical, 2·5-6·5 cm. long, 3-5 mm. broad, linear, with an acute callous at the apex, attenuated at the base, somewhat channelled above, hispid on the upper surface, woolly-canescent beneath except on the midrib, entire, spinulose-ciliate. *Heads* many to each root. *Peduncle* about 3·5 cm. long, sparsely woolly, especially beneath the involucre, or subglabrous. *Involucral-tube* 7 mm. long, 6 mm. in diameter, turbinate; lobes in 4 rows; outer lobes 6 mm. long, 1 mm. broad, linear, obtuse, spinulose-ciliate; inner lobes 4 mm. long, 2 mm. broad, ovate, obtuse with reddish-brown membranous margins. *Ray-florets* neuter, white with a purplish band beneath; corolla tube 7 mm. long, cylindric; limb 1·7 mm. long, 4·5 mm. broad, lanceolate, bifid at the apex, with each lobe minutely 2-toothed, about 7-nerved and distinctly 2-keeled beneath. *Disc-florets* hermaphrodite; corolla-tube 6 mm. long, subcylindric, somewhat 5-angled, glabrous; lobes 1·5 mm. long, ·5 mm. broad, lanceolate, obtuse. *Pappus* of hyaline linear scales 1·5 mm. long. *Ovary* covered with long silky hairs; style 7 mm. long, cylindric (lengthening with age); stigmas ·75 long, linear, obtuse.

PLATE 64.—Fig. 1, young flower head; Fig. 2, section through involucre; Fig. 3, flower head just before opening; Fig. 4, surface view of flower head; Fig. 5, corolla of ray-florets; Fig. 6, disc floret; Fig. 7, leaf; all variously enlarged.

F.P.S.A., 1922.

K.A. LANSDELL DEL.

PLATE 65.

LILIACEAE. TRIBE SCILLEAE.

Ornithogalum, Linn.; Benth. et Hook. f. Gen. Plant.
Ornithogalum Thunbergianum, *Baker in Journ. Linn. Soc.*

Ornithogalum Thunbergianum, the "Yellow Chinkerichee," is found in the Malmesbury, Paarl, and Van Rhynsdorp Districts of Cape Province. It was found by Carl Thunberg at Saldana Bay about the year 1772, and named by him *O. maculatum*, but as this specific name had already been given to a plant figured by Jacquin, the late Mr. Baker redescribed the species here dealt with and named it after Thunberg, although there is some doubt as to whether the plant figured by Jacquin is specifically distinct from *O. Thunbergianum*.

The perianth is a beautiful "flame scarlet" colour with a black mark at the tip of the three outer segments. The species should be grown by all lovers of our native flora, and would well repay cultivation.

We are indebted to Mrs. E. Rood, Van Rhynsdorp, for specimens which enabled us to prepare the present plate. Specimens are preserved in the National Herbarium, Pretoria (Herb. No. 1469).

DESCRIPTION:—*Bulb* 2-3 cm. long, 2-3 cm. in diameter, ovoid or compressed-globose, covered with thin membranous tunics. *Leaves* withering at time of flowering, 5-10 cm. long, 1 cm. broad below, ovate-linear, tapering to an acute apex, glabrous, glaucous-green. *Peduncle* 12-38 cm. long, terete, rigid, glabrous. *Inflorescence* 2-6-flowered. *Bracts* membranous, 2·3-2·5 cm. long, linear-oblong, acuminate, more or less clasping and equalling the pedicel. *Pedicels* 1·7 cm. long, terete, the lower somewhat arcuate. *Perianth segments* 2-2·3 long, ·8-1 cm. broad; the outer obovate-oblanceolate, subacute, with a black mark at the apex; the inner ovate-lanceolate. *Filaments* 7 mm. long, cylindric, slightly narrowing above; anthers 3 mm. long. *Ovary* 8 mm. long, 5 mm. in diameter, ellipsoid; style 2 mm. long; stigma trigonous.

PLATE 65.—Fig. 1, stamens; Fig. 2, gynaecium; Fig. 3, bract.

F.P.S.A., 1922.

K. A. LANSDELL DEL.

PLATE 66.

FERRARIA ANTHEROSA.
Cape Province.

IRIDACEAE. TRIBE MOROEEAE.

FERRARIA, Linn.; Benth. et Hook. f. Gen. Plant.
Ferraria antherosa, *Ker. in Bot. Mag. 751; Fl.*

Our species was first figured in Curtis' *Botanical Magazine* in 1804 from a plant which was raised in Salisbury's garden at Brompton, England. It is not at all a well-known plant, as it is only recorded in the *Flora Capensis* as having been collected by Zeyher in the Clanwilliam District, and by Ecklon at Groenkloof in the Malmesbury District. The plant from which our plate was prepared was sent to the Division of Botany, Pretoria, by Mrs. E. Rood from Van Rhynsdorp. The genus *Ferraria* is represented in South Africa by six species, and by one species in Angola. The flowers last only for a very short time after opening, but a succession of flowers appears on each plant. None of the species can be called ornamental from a gardener's point of view, but the structure of the flower is very beautiful and the colouring quaint. Plants would only be grown as a botanical curiosity, and not for their beauty. Specimens are preserved in the National Herbarium, Pretoria (Herb. No. 1471).

DESCRIPTION:—*Corms* several arranged one on top of the other, discoid, about 3·5 cm. in diameter. *Plant* about 23 cm. high. *Leaves* three, 17-26 cm. long, linear and 1 cm. broad above, subacute, equitant and clasping the stem below. *Bracts* subtending the inflorescences, resembling the leaves. *Bracts* subtending the ultimate inflorescence 5-8 cm. long, 1·6-2·6 cm. broad, elliptic, boat-shaped, with membranous margins. *Perianth segments* 2·5 cm. long, forming a campanulate portion 1·5 cm. long and 1·3 cm. in diameter, then spreading into a horizontal portion; the spreading portion 1·4 cm. long, 1·4 broad, ovate, subacute, with frilled margins. *Staminal tube* 1·6 cm. long, cylindric, anther lobes diverging. *Ovary* cylindric, with a beak 3 cm. long; stigmas long-fimbriated.

PLATE 66.—Fig. 1, corms; Fig. 2, flower; Fig. 3, top of style showing stigmas and anthers; Fig. 4, stigma.

F.P.S.A., 1922.

K. A. LANSDELL DEL.

PLATE 67.

HARVEYA SQUAMOSA.

Cape Province, Natal, Little Namaqualand.

Scrophulariaceae. Tribe Gerardieae.

Harveya, Hook.; Benth. et Hook. f. Gen. Plant.

Harveya squamosa, *Steud. Nomencl. Bot. ed. 2, i. 723: Fl.*

The Genus *Harveya* contains 27 species, all of which are parasitic on the roots of other plants. In South Africa 21 species are recorded, the remainder being found in Tropical Africa and the Mascarene Islands. The name was given by Sir William Hooker in commemoration of Dr. Harvey, who was one of the pioneers of South African systematic botany. The plant belongs to a group known as total parasites, *i.e.* it is wholly dependent on its host for its food supply. Specialised roots technically known as "haustoria" penetrate the roots of the host plant and absorb the requisite food material.

The species here figured occurs in the Cape Peninsula, all along the western coastal districts to Clanwilliam and Van Rhynsdorp and into Little Namaqualand. It has also been recorded from the sand-dunes near Durban in Natal. The specimens from which our plate was prepared were collected by Mrs. E. Rood at Van Rhynsdorp, and are preserved in the National Herbarium, Pretoria (Herb. No. 1456).

Description:—A herbaceous plant about 13 cm. high. *Scale leaves* 8 mm. long, 1 cm. broad, ovate, acuminate, pubescent without. *Inflorescence* racemose, densely many-flowered, 2·5 cm. in diameter, more or less cylindric; axis 1 cm. in diameter near base, narrowing upwards. *Bracts* 1-2 cm. long, ·5-·9 cm. broad, oblong or obovate-spathulate, obtuse, glandular pilose without; bracteoles 2, opposite at base of the calyx, 3 cm. long, 1·5 mm. broad, linear, glandular-pilose. *Pedicels* 1 cm. long, fleshy. *Calyx-tube* 2·5 cm. long, 7 mm. in diameter, tubular, glandular-pilose without, glabrous within; lobes 1·5-1·7 cm. long, 3 mm. broad at the base, gradually tapering from a triangular base. *Corolla-tube* 3 cm. long, 4 mm. in diameter, tubular, glandular-pilose without and also within about the middle; lobes 4 mm. long, 5 mm. broad, semiorbicular, rounded above, somewhat concave, glandular-pubescent without. *Stamens* attached to the middle of the corolla tube; filaments of 2 different lengths; the longer 1·6 cm. long; the shorter 1·3 cm. long; all sparsely covered with glandular hairs; anthers with one fertile lobe and one unfertile lobe. *Ovary* 5 mm. long, 4 mm. in diameter; style 2·5 cm. long, terete, sparsely covered with a few glandular hairs; stigma clavate, faintly 2-lobed.

PLATE 67.—Fig. 1, showing haustoria attached to portion of host; Fig. 2, single flowers showing bract and bracteoles; Fig. 3, bract; Fig. 4, bracteole; Fig. 5, calyx laid open; Fig. 6, corolla; Fig. 7, corolla laid open; Fig. 8, stigma; Figs. 9, 10, portion of filaments with anther; Fig. 11, style and ovary.

F.P.S.A., 1922.

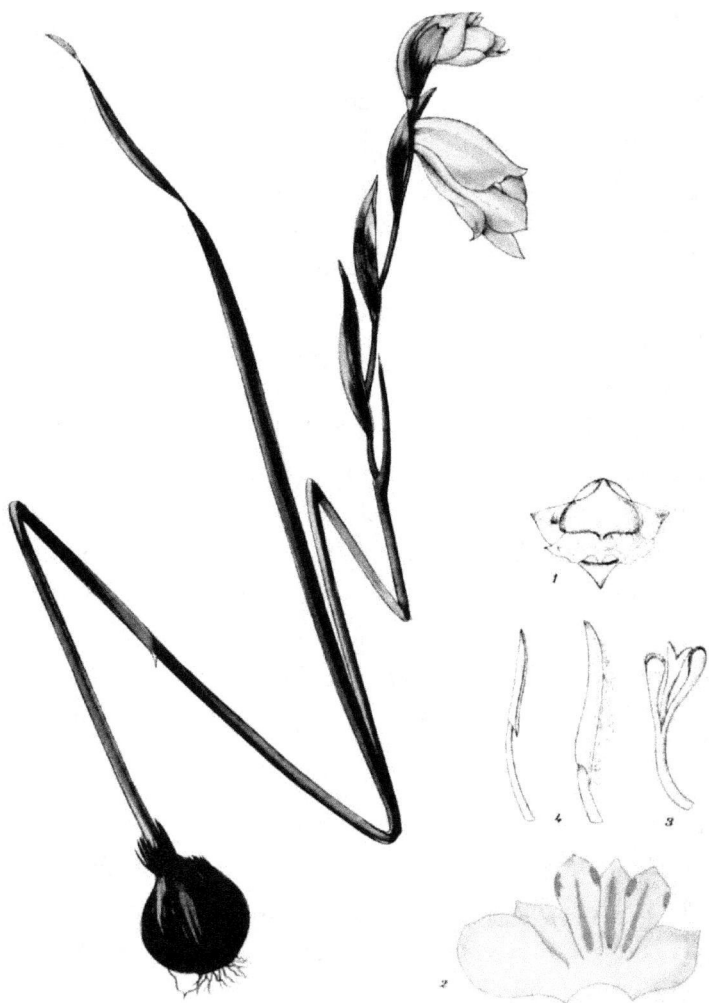

K. A. LANSDELL DEL.

PLATE 68.

GLADIOLUS P<small>RITZELII</small>.

Cape Province.

I<small>RIDEAE</small>. T<small>RIBE</small> I<small>XIEAE</small>.

G<small>LADIOLUS</small>, Linn.; Benth. et Hook. f. Gen. Plant.
Gladiolus Pritzelii, *Diels in Engl. Bot. Jahrb.*

This graceful little *Gladiolus* was first found by Diels at Hantams Berg, Calvinia District, and described by him in 1909, and in September 1921 the plant was again collected by Dr. R. Marloth in the same locality. It belongs to the same group in the genus as *G. spathaceus* (the Caledon Bluebell), and *G. involutus* (the George Bluebell), having the same bell-shaped flowers. In the original description the plant is said to be one-flowered, but in the specimens received from Dr. Marloth the spikes were 2-4-flowered.

Specimens are preserved in the National Herbarium, Pretoria (Herb. No. 1459).

D<small>ESCRIPTION</small>:—*Corm* globose, 2 cm. long, 2·2 cm. in diameter, with fibrous tunics produced into a short neck. *Leaves* two to each plant; the lower about 5 cm. long, spathaceous, clasping the stem, minutely pubescent and with hyaline margins; the upper 26-43 cm. long, free for 14-24 cm. above, linear, acute, with two prominent ribs above and beneath. *Spikes* 2-4-flowered. *Outer spathe valve* membranous, 3 cm. long, 8 mm. broad, lanceolate, many-veined, with membranous margins, glabrous; inner valve 2 cm. long, hyaline-membranous. *Perianth-tube* 7 mm.

long, curved, cylindric below, becoming campanulate above. *Posterior-lobes* 1·5 cm. long, 1 cm. broad, obovate, subacuminate, obtuse; anterior lobe 2·3 cm. long, 1·3 cm. broad, obovate, rounded above, hooded; side lobes 1·5 cm. long, 1·3 cm. broad, obovate, shortly and bluntly acuminate. *Anthers* projecting beyond the junction with the filament. *Ovary* 3 mm. long, ellipsoid; style terete; stigmas spathulate, 2-lobed.

PLATE 68.—Fig. 1, front view of flower; Fig. 2, perianth laid open; Fig. 3, upper part of style, showing stigmas; Fig. 4, anthers.

F.P.S.A., 1922.

69.

S GOWER DEL.

PLATE 69.

GAZANIA PAVONIA.
Cape Province.

COMPOSITAE. TRIBE ARCTOTIDEAE.

GAZANIA, Gaertn.; Benth. et Hook. f. Gen. Plant.
Gazania Pavonia, *R. Br. in Ait. Hort. Kew. 2.*

This extremely handsome species of *Gazania* was cultivated by Mr. C. N. Knox-Davies in Johannesburg from plants collected at Worcester in the Cape Province. The plants form a dense mass, and are suitable either for growing in a border or in large pots. The ray florets are a beautiful nopal red, with a warm sepia-brown eye-spot at the base, and when the plants are in full bloom they present a very striking appearance. It is surprising that species of this genus, which are amongst the most handsome of the South African Compositae, have received so little attention from horticulturists, and though hundreds of our native plants have been figured in the *Botanical Magazine* only two species of Gazania have been illustrated.

Mr. N. E. Brown, who contributed an account of the genus to *The Garden*, wrote that "it is one of the most perplexing that a botanist has to deal with," and even to-day the species are very imperfectly known. Our plant was submitted to Kew for verification of the name, and the Director reports, "The *Gazania* has not been exactly matched, but might be regarded as a form of *G. Pavonia, R. Br.*"

Specimens are preserved in the National Herbarium, Pretoria (Herb. No. 1473).

DESCRIPTION:—*Plant* compact, decumbent, forming a clump about 30 cm. in diameter. *Leaves* crowded near the apex of short shoots, 6-10 cm. long, pinnatisect, slightly broadened and clasping at the base; lobes 1-2·5 cm. long, 2·5-4 mm. broad, linear, subacute, woolly-tomentose beneath except on the mid-rib, sparsely woolly above, at length becoming glabrous. *Peduncle* 9 mm. long, terete, sparsely woolly, at length becoming glabrous. *Tube of involucre* 9 mm. long, 8 mm. in diameter, sparsely woolly, intruse at the base; lobes in three rows; the outer 4 mm. long, less than 1 mm. broad, linear, subacute; the innermost ovate, subacuminate, subobtuse, with reddish-brown margins. *Ray-florets* neuter, corolla tube 7 mm. long, cylindric; limb red with a dark-coloured mark at the base, 1·9 cm. long, 8 mm. broad, obovate, rounded and minutely 3-fid at the apex, with two prominent veins beneath. *Disc-florets* hermaphrodite. *Corolla-tube* 7 mm. long, more or less angled, glabrous; lobes ·5 mm. long, ovate, subacute. *Anthers* 3 mm. long. *Pappus* of long delicate linear scales connate in the lower half and encasing the base of the corolla tube, free in the upper half. *Ovary* densely clothed with long silky hairs; style elongating up to 1·3 cm. long, filiform; stigmas about 0·75 mm. long.

PLATE 69.—Fig. 1, limb of ray flower; Fig. 2, longitudinal section of involucre; Fig. 3, ray flower; Fig. 4, segment of leaf enlarged.

F.P.S.A., 1922.

K A LANSDELL DEL.

PLATE 70.

Ochnaceae. Tribe Ochnaceae.

Ochna, Schreb.; Benth. et Hook. f. Gen. Plant.

Ochna pretoriensis, *Phillips*, sp. nov. *Rami* glabri. *Folia* 1·5-3·8 cm. longa, 0·5-1·7 cm. lata, lanceolata, obovata, elliptica vel oblanceolata, apice obtusa, basi cuneata, marginibus serratis. *Flores* solitarii vel 2-nati. *Pedicelli* 1-1·5 cm. longi, basi articulati. *Sepala* 7-8 mm. longa, 4·5 mm. lata, ovata vel elliptica, apice rotundata, aliquando 2-3-lobata. *Petala* 1·5 cm. longa, 9·5 mm. lata, obovata, apice rotundata, basi unguiculata. *Filamenta* 4·5 mm. longa, apice articulata. *Ovarium* 4-5-loculare; stylus 5 mm. longus, apice 4-5-lobatus.

This *Ochna*, which is found in the Transvaal around Pretoria and at Messina, has hitherto been confused with *O. atropurpurea*, but is easily distinguished from that species by the larger more expanded flowers and the non-pustulate branches. The latter character distinguishes *O. atropurpurea* from all the other South African species of the genus.

Our plate was prepared from specimens collected on Meintjes Kop, Pretoria, by Mr. D. J. Fouche in September, 1921. It is a low spreading bush, and at this time of the year is one mass of sweet-smelling yellow flowers. The leaves do not appear until December or January, and it is then that the green sepals enlarge and turn a blood-red colour and surround the black fruit. The plant, therefore, either in flower or fruit makes a very ornamental shrub and well worth the attention of cultivators.

The genus *Ochna* contains several species producing valuable timber.

Specimens are preserved in the National Herbarium, Pretoria (Herb. Nos. 1422, 1491).

DESCRIPTION:—*Branches* with light to dark brown bark, peeling off in membranous strips, not pustulate. *Leaves* 1·5-3·8 cm. long, ·5-1·7 cm. broad, lanceolate, obovate, elliptic, or oblanceolate (mostly oblanceolate), obtuse at the apex, cuneate or more rarely rounded at the base, with serrated margins and with the mid-rib distinct and the lateral veins evident. *Flowers* solitary, very rarely paired, arising at the apex of abbreviated shoots. *Pedicels* 1-1·5 cm. long, articulated at or 1-2 mm. above the base. *Sepals* 7-8 mm. long, 4-5 mm. broad, ovate or elliptic, rounded at and sometimes 2-8-lobed at the apex, enlarging in the fruit. *Petals* 1·5 cm. long, 9·5 mm. broad, obovate, rounded at the apex, narrowed at the base into a claw. *Filaments* 4·5 mm. long, articulated at the apex; anthers 2 mm. long, oblong. *Ovary* of 4-6 carpels; style 5 mm. long; stigmas as many as the carpels. *Fruit* 7-8 mm. long, 5-6 mm. broad, more or less ellipsoid.

PLATE 70.—Fig. 1, fruiting branch; Fig. 2, flower with petals removed; Fig. 3, sepal; Fig. 4, petal; Figs. 5 and 6, stamens; Fig. 7, gynaecium.

F.P.S.A., 1922.

71.

S GOWER DEL.

PLATE 71.

DAUBENYA AUREA, var. COCCINEA.
Cape Province.

LILIACEAE. TRIBE ALLIEAE.

DAUBENYA, Lindl.; Benth. et Hook. f. Gen. Plant.
Daubenya aurea, *Lindl., var.* **coccinea**, *Marloth comb. nov.*
Daubenya coccinea, Harv. Fl.

This rare and interesting plant was found by Dr. R. Marloth in the Calvinia District. An examination of fresh specimens has enabled us to reduce the three species described in the "Flora Capensis" to a single species, and the genus *Daubenya* therefore becomes one of South Africa's monotypic genera. Our conclusions have been confirmed by independent observations made by Dr. Marloth, and we give below the notes he forwarded to the Division of Botany.

"The colour of the flower is the most brilliant scarlet known in the Flora of South Africa, and especially dazzling when seen in full sunlight. This effect is due to the combination of two pigments in the subepidermal tissues of the flower, viz. a granular yellow pigment distributed through all the cells, and a bright red solution present in most of the cells of the subepidermal layer, but absent in others. This peculiarity of structure also explains the occurrence of plants with yellow flowers, for if through some cause or other (as a sport), the red pigment is not produced, the flower is plain yellow, just as in such a case the flower of the red *Watsonia* (*W. rosa*) becomes pure white (Arderne's Watsonia). It so happened that the yellow form was first introduced into England and described by Lindley as *Daubenya aurea* (1835), hence this name has to be retained for the species, although the flower is generally scarlet, and the yellow form has only arisen as a sport. There is, however, no structural difference between *D. aurea* Lindl., *D. coccinea* Harv., and *D. fulva* Lindl."

The length of the floral segments and of the peduncle, given as distinguishing characters by Lindley, is very variable in the specimens seen by us (over one hundred); some of them are scarlet, others yellow, and some dull orange. The scent of the flowers is unpleasant, somewhat recalling that of the flowers of *Rhus*.

The home of this remarkable plant was unknown to botanists until re-discovered in 1920. It grows in heavy red clay soil on the farm Fransplaas, about 40 miles north of Sutherland, and flowers in September.

The genus was named by Dr. Lindley in honour of Dr. Charles Daubeny, Professor of Botany at Oxford, "whose interesting researches in vegetable Chemistry have materially conduced to improve our knowledge of the physiology of plants."

Specimens are preserved in the National Herbarium, Pretoria (Herb. No. 1458).

DESCRIPTION:—An acaulescent herbaceous plant. *Bulb* 1·6 cm. long, 1·9 cm. in diameter, covered with brown membranous tunics with numerous fibrous roots from the base. *Leaves* 2, flat, 5-8 cm. long, 4-5 cm. broad, ovate, subacuminate, obtuse, narrowed and clasping at the base, many-nerved, with margins narrowly membranous. *Capitulum* about 10-flowered, with a peduncle 3 cm. long, clasped by the leaf base and beneath the soil. *Outer bracts* white, membranous, 2·7 cm. long, 1·6 cm. broad, oblong; inner bracts 2·5 cm. long, 9 mm. broad, obovate-spathulate, entire, clasping the perianth-tube. *Pedicels* 5 mm. long,

3 mm. broad, compressed, fleshy. *The outer flowers* 2-lipped and differently shaped from the inner. *Perianth-tube* of outer flowers 2 cm. long, 4 mm. in diameter, somewhat compressed; lobes of lower lip 2·6 cm. long; the middle lobe 1·4 cm. broad; the 2 side lobes 1 cm. broad; all obovate-oblong, obtuse; lobes of upper lip 3 mm. long, 1 mm. broad, linear. *Perianth-lobes* of inner flowers 3-6 mm. long, all linear or lanceolate. *Stamens* inserted at different levels; filaments 3-6 mm. long, terete, fleshy, tapering upwards; anthers 2 mm. long, oblong. *Ovary* 7 mm. long, 2·5 mm. in diameter, narrowly ellipsoid, glabrous; style 2·5 cm. long, terete, with 3 minute stigmas at the apex.

PLATE 71.—Fig. 1, plant viewed from above; Fig. 2, plant, side view; Fig. 3, a single flower; Fig. 4, side view of flower of outer whorl; Fig. 5, flower from middle of inflorescence; Fig. 6, the same flower viewed from above, showing the stamens and style; Fig. 7, bract.

F.P.S.A., 1922.

K A LANSDELL DEL.

PLATE 72.

STAPELIA PILLANSII, var. ATTENUATA.
Cape Province.

ASCLEPIADACEAE. TRIBE STAPELIEAE.

STAPELIA, Linn.; Benth. et Hook. f. Gen. Plant.
Stapelia Pillansii, *N. E. Br.*, var. **attenuata**, *N. E. Br. in Fl.*

This interesting *Stapelia* was first discovered by Mr. N. S. Pillans, of Cape Town, at Witte Poort in the Laingsburg Division, and described by Mr. N. E. Brown, to whom Mr. Pillans sent most of his collections of this group. Our plant is one of the larger-flowered species of the genus, resembling in this respect *S. gigantea* and *S. nobilis*, but differing in colour from both these species. The flowers have a distinct carrion-like odour, although this is not so strong as in many other species of the genus. When in bud the petals form an acuminate beak recurved at the apex. Under cultivation in the greenhouse the stems turn a dark reddish-brown colour.

Our specimen was collected by Dr. I. B. Pole Evans at Laingsburg, and flowered at the Division of Botany, Pretoria, in October, 1921. (National Herbarium, Pretoria, Herb. No. 1492.)

DESCRIPTION:—*Stems* 9-15 cm. high, 1·4-2·2 cm. in diameter, 4-angled and with concave sides, pubescent, usually green. *Teeth* with erect whitish rudimentary leaves about 2 mm. long. *Flowers* 2 (4 or 5 according to Brown) from near the base of the stems. *Pedicels* 3-4 cm. long, terete, pubescent. *Sepals* 1·7 cm. long, 2 mm. broad at the base, linear-lanceolate, acuminate, acute, pubescent.

Corolla when expanded 22·5 cm. in diameter, diamine-brown above, smooth and without markings, glabrous; lobes 10·5 cm. long, 2·2 cm. broad at the base, ovate, tapering to a long point, strongly revolute, ciliate with short hairs and with longer vibratile hairs. *Corona* dark coloured; outer corona lobes 4 mm. long, 2 mm. broad, oblong, bluntly 3-lobed at the apex; the middle lobe the largest; inner corona-lobes 7 mm. long, 3 mm. broad, obovate, flattened and appearing to stand at right angles to the outer lobes, on either edge produced into a beak; the inner beak longer than the outer and recurved over the flattened portion of the corona; the outer beak entire or irregularly 2-3-lobed.

PLATE 72.—Fig. 1, corona; Fig. 2, lobe of inner corona; Fig. 3, lobe of *outer corona*.

F.P.S.A., 1922.

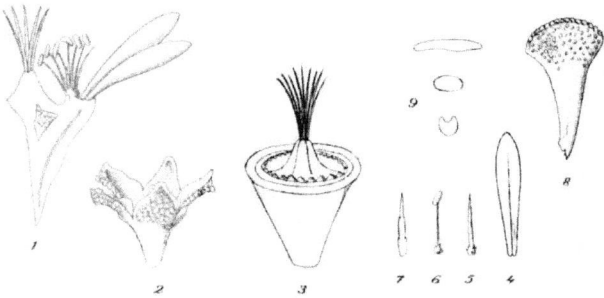

M M Page del

M. M. PAGE DEL.

PLATE 73.

MESEMBRYANTHEMUM CRASSIPES.

Cape Province.

FICOIDEAE. TRIBE MESEMBRYEAE.

MESEMBRYANTHEMUM, Linn.; Benth. et Hook. f. Gen. Plant. vol. i. p. 853.

Mesembryanthemum crassipes, *Marloth*, sp. nov. habitu *M. rosulati* (Kensit in Trans. Roy. Soc. S. Afr. i. p. 155, pi. xxib) et *M. calcarei*, Marl. (Flora of S. A. vol. i. pl. 52) sed foliis cuneatis aspero-marginatis et floribus roseis 5-meris distincta.

Planta subacaulis, ramis paucis brevissimis e radice crasso carnoso ramoso. *Folia* in rosulam aggregata, plana, cuneata, crassa, suberecta, apice retusa vel rotundata, apicem versus margineque tuberculis minutis griseis numerosis munita. *Flores* apice ramulorum solitarii. *Calyx* 5-fidus, lobis subaequalibus triangularibus, colore griseo foliorum. *Petala* lanceolata, uniseriata, saturate rosea. *Stamina* incarnata basin versus barbata. *Stigmata* 8-10, filiformia, staminibus aequilonga.

This is a beautiful plant when in flower, owing to the contrast between the deep pink petals and the rugose grey leaves. It was collected on a stony plain of grey shale near Sutherland, at an altitude of 4600 feet, by Dr. R. Marloth, and flowered in his garden at Cape Town in September, 1921.

DESCRIPTION:—*Root* thick, fleshy, simple or branched up to 30 mm. in diam. and 20 cm. long. *Stem* none, but one or more short branches arising from the crown of the caudex. *Leaves* crowded, 6-10 on a branch, mostly erect and exposing the margin to the midday sun, cuneate, gradually narrowed to the base, the apex straight or slightly rounded, occasionally with a blunt mucro; the apical portion, and especially the apical margin, closely covered with fine tubercles; on the wild plant the entire leaf greyish-green, the margin reddish. *Flowers* solitary on each branch, sessile or subsessile, supported by 2 connate leaf-like bracts. *Calyx* turbiniform, 10-12 mm. long, the tube 11-13 mm. in diam. at the mouth; sepals 5, of which 3 nearly equal, the 2 others narrower, all triangular, 10 mm. long and wide, with a very narrow hyaline margin and a thick umbo below the apex, finely tuberculate like the leaves, grey, the margin red. *Petals* uniseriate, narrow-lanceolate or spathulate, 13-14 mm. long and 2-2·5 mm. wide in the middle, deep pink on the inner side, paler on the outer side. *Stamens* white, bending inwards near the base and then erect, bearded at the bend. *Styles* 8-10, filiform, 6 mm. long, arising from the apex of the conical ovary. Total diam. of open flower 20-25 mm., opening in the sun and closing towards evening for several days.

PLATE 73.—Fig. 1, longitudinal section through the flower; Fig. 2, calyx; Fig. 3, gynaecium; Figs. 4, 5, 6, 7, petals and stamen; Fig. 8, entire leaf; Fig. 9, cross-sections of leaf.

F.P.S.A., 1922.

74.

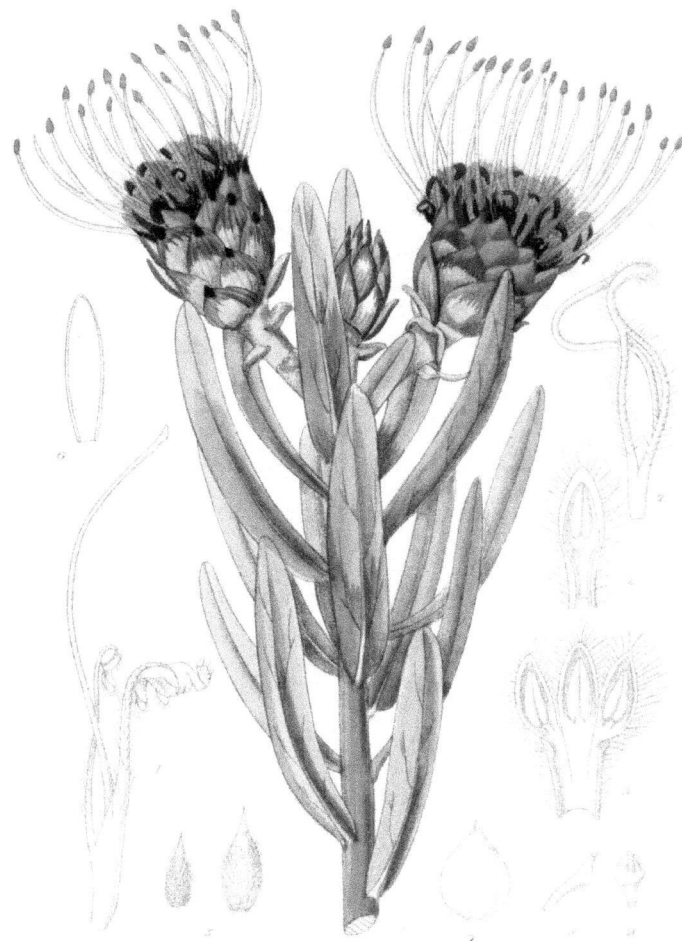

S GOWER DEL.

PLATE 74.

LEUCOSPERMUM TOTTUM, var. GLABRUM.
Cape Province.

PROTEACEAE. TRIBE PROTEEAE.

LEUCOSPERMUM, R. Br.; Benth. et Hook. f. Gen. Plant.
Leucospermum tottum, *R. Br., var.* **glabrum**, *Phillips,*
var. nov. a typo ramis glabris, bracteis eciliatis differt.

This interesting *Leucospermum* was collected by Mr. T. P. Stokoe in Jan du Toit's Kloof near Chavonnesberg, in the Western Province. Mr. Stokoe states that only a few plants were observed growing in a belt of *Proteaceae.* It is evidently very closely related to *L. tottum,* from which it differs in having glabrous branches and non-ciliate involucral bracts, and should be regarded as a glabrous variety of this species. The genus *Leucospermum* is closely related to *Protea* (see plate 22) but differs from that genus in having the limb of the posticous segment divided and not completely fused. The well-known "Kreupelboom" (*L. concospermum*) belongs to this genus.

The variety here figured might be regarded as one of the more striking plants in the genus *Leucospermum.* The yellow styles with red stigmas projecting from an involucre tinged with delicate shades of red and green give a particularly pleasing effect.

Specimens are preserved in the National Herbarium, Pretoria (Herb. No. 1493).

DESCRIPTION:—A spreading bush 5-6 ft. high. *Branches* glabrous. *Leaves* 8-8·5 cm. long, O·9-1 cm. broad, broadly linear,

3-toothed at the apex, slightly narrowed at the base with the midrib distinct beneath, veins faint above. *Heads* solitary or 2-nate, 7-8 cm. long including the peduncle and styles, about 5·5 cm. in diameter. *Peduncle* 2 cm. long, loosely covered with ovate subacuminate obtuse glabrous bracts 8 mm. long and about 8 mm. broad. *Receptacle* 2·2 cm. long, 7 mm. broad, cylindric, densely villous on the back with long white hairs. *Perianth-tube* 1 cm. long, glabrous; segments 2·5 cm. long, linear, villous and long ciliate; lobes 3 mm. long, oblong, subacuminate, ciliate and bearded. *Ovary* 1 mm. long, villous; style 4·5 cm. long, terete, glabrous; stigma ovoid, subacuminate, obtuse.

PLATE 74.—Fig. 1, a single flower; Fig. 2, flower bud; Fig. 3, limb of posticous segment; Fig. 4, one lobe of limb showing stamen; Fig. 5, floral bracts; Fig. 6, longitudinal section of receptacle; Fig. 7, involucral bract; Fig. 8, stigma, side view; Fig. 9, stigma, front view.

F.P.S.A., 1922.

S GOWER DEL.

PLATE 75.

LILIACEAE. TRIBE SCILLEAE.

ORNITHOGALUM, Linn.; Benth. et Hook. f. Gen. Plant.

Ornithogalum Roodeae, *Phillips*, sp. nov. *Bulbus* globosus, albus. *Folia* 3, ad 26 cm. longa, basi 2·5 cm. lata, lanceolata, acuminata, glabra. *Pedunculus* ad 25 cm. longus, glaber. *Inflorescentia* 4 cm. longa, circiter 6 cm. lata. *Bracteae* 1·4-2·5 cm. longae, ovato-lanceolatae, acuminatae, membranaceae. *Pedicelli* 1·1-2·5 cm. longi. *Segmenta* perianthii 1·2 cm. longa, 4 mm. lata, oblongo-lanceolata, apice papillosa. *Filamenta* 8 mm. longa, basi 1·5 lata, lanceolata, acuminata. *Ovarium* 5 mm. longum, 2.5 mm. latum, glabrum; stylus 6 mm. longus; stigma semiglobosum, papillosum.

This handsome *Ornithogalum* was collected by Mr. E. Rood at Van Rhynsdorp, and forwarded to the Division of Botany, Pretoria. The perianth segments are a deep reddish-brown, edged with white, and the flowers are extremely fragrant. Specimens were sent to Kew, and the Director reports that the plant had not been matched, the nearest affinity being *O. suaveolens*, Jacq., and that it was evidently a new species. This species exhibits a device for cross-pollination by the movement of the style. As soon as the flower opens the style bends downwards, and is thus in a position to receive pollen from the abdomen of a visiting insect. As the flowers wither the perianth segments close up, and the style becomes erect and would then be self-pollinated if cross-pollination has not taken place.

DESCRIPTION:—*Bulb* 2·2 cm. long, 2·8 cm. in diameter, globose, white. *Leaves* 3, up to 26 cm. long, 2·5 cm. broad at the base, lanceolate (when opened flat), becoming deeply channelled above, acuminate, clasping at the base, glabrous. *Peduncle* up to 25 cm. long, greenish-brown, glabrous. *Infloresence* about 14-flowered, more or less corymbose, 4 mm. long, about 6 cm. in diameter. *Bracts* 1·4-2·5 cm. long, ovate-lanceolate, acuminate into a long fine point, membranous, as long as the pedicels. *Pedicels* 1·1-2·5 cm. long, terete. *Perianth-segments* free to the base, spreading, 1·2 cm. long, 4 mm. broad, oblong-lanceolate, dark purple with white margins, 5-nerved; the outer cucullate at the apex with a fringe of short glandular hairs; the inner rounded and fringed with short glandular hairs. *Filaments* 8 mm. long, 1·5 mm. broad in widest part, lanceolate, acuminate, more or less compressed below, convex on both sides above; anthers 4 mm. long, oblong, each lobe with a short beak. *Ovary* 5 mm. long, 2·5 mm. in diameter, 3-lobed, glabrous; style 6 mm. long, semiterete; the style in open flowers bent away from stamens and later becoming sharply bent; stigma semiglobose, covered with glandular hairs.

PLATE 75.—Fig. 1, flower; Fig. 2, bract; Fig. 3, stamen; Fig. 4, cross-section of ovary; Fig. 5, gynaecium; Fig. 6, outer perianth-segments, front and side views; Fig. 7, inner perianth-segments, front and side views.

F.P.S.A., 1922.

K. A. LANSDELL DEL.

PLATE 76.

PROTEA RECONDITA.
Cape Province.

PROTEACEAE. TRIBE PROTEEAE.

PROTEA, Linn.; Benth. et Hook. f. Gen. Plant.
Protea recondita, *Buek. ex Meisn. in DC. Prodr. xiv. 237; Fl.*

This rare *Protea* was sent to us by Miss L. Guthrie of the Bolus Herbarium, who received it from Mr. de Wet of Ceres. Mr. de Wet described it as a low trailing plant with the branches 2 feet long and raised about a foot above the ground. The heads are hidden by the upper leaves. Hitherto the species has only been recorded from Ezelsbank on the Cedarberg Range, Clanwilliam Division, where it was collected by Drège almost a hundred years ago.

This example, unlike so many species of *Protea*, is not particularly handsome. The bracts are a pale dull green, and the flowers somewhat scented, reminding one very much of the odour of *Protea mellifera*.

Specimens are preserved in the National Herbarium, Pretoria (Herb. No. 1490).

DESCRIPTION:—*Branches* pale green, glabrous. *Leaves* 7-19 cm. long, 1·8-7 cm. broad (the largest leaves surrounding the head), elliptic or elliptic-lanceolate, obtuse, narrowed to the base, with distinct reddish veins and a reddish margin, glabrous. *Head* sessile, 5·5 cm. long, 7 cm. in diameter. *Involucral-bracts* in about 9 rows; the outer ovate, subacuminate, obtuse, ciliate; the inner oblong, incurved, somewhat concave, slightly exceeding the flowers, scantily pilose. *Receptacle* 3·2 cm. broad at base, about 1·5 cm. high, conical. *Perianth-sheath* 2·6 cm. long, dilated, keeled and 3-nerved below, glabrous, except for setae near the apex; lip 6 mm. long, setulose with golden-brown hairs. *Hypogynous scales* 1·5 mm. long, ovate. *Ovary* covered with long golden-brown hairs; style 4 cm. long, strongly falcate; stigma 3 mm. long, almost imperceptibly passing into the style.

PLATE 76.—Fig. 1, branch with flower head; Fig. 2, receptacle; Fig. 3, inner bract; Fig. 4, outer bract; Fig. 5, single flower; Fig. 6, one perianthlobe.

F.P.S.A., 1922.

77.

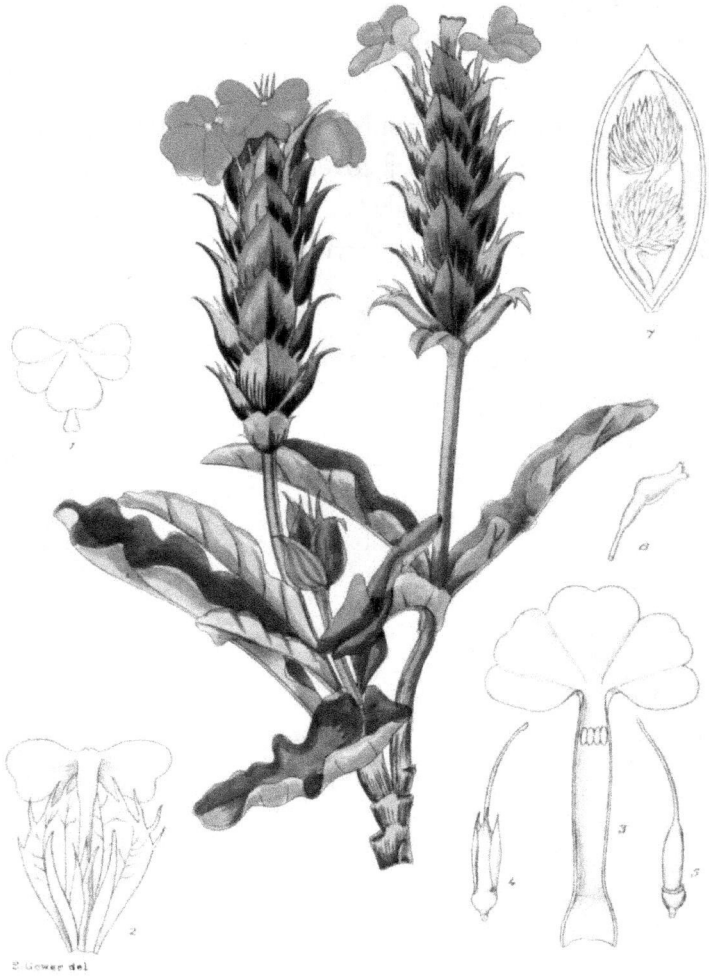

S. GOWER DEL.

PLATE 77.

CROSSANDRA Greenstockii.
Transvaal, Natal.

Acanthaceae. Tribe Justicieae.

Crossandra, Salisb.; Benth. et Hook. f. Gen Plant.
Crossandra Greenstockii, *S. Moore in Journ. Bot.*

This plant is of interest as being one of the many outliers of the Tropical African flora in Southern Africa, and also as showing a connection between the floras of Eastern India and Tropical Africa. The genus *Crossandra* is represented by about 15 species, most of which occur in Tropical Africa, and one is recorded from India and the Malay States. The species figured here occurs in the Nyasa Highlands, and extends into Natal and the Transvaal as far south as Pretoria. During the month of October the plant may be found in flower in the neighbourhood of the Premier Mine, Pretoria, and the bright scarlet flowers form a conspicuous feature in the veld. Specimens have been recorded from various localities in the Northern Transvaal.

The fruits, as is so frequent in many species of *Acanthaceae*, have an explosive mechanism, *i.e.* they burst suddenly into two valves when wetted and scatter the seeds. The seeds, of which there are four in each fruit, are tightly enveloped with long hairs which straighten out and become mucilaginous when wet, thus fixing the seed to the ground.

Specimens are preserved in the National Herbarium, Pretoria (Herb. No. 1494).

DESCRIPTION:—An acaulescent plant with underground rootstocks. *Stem* short, glabrous. *Leaves* opposite, 5-11 cm. long, 2·2-5·2 cm. broad, obovate or elliptic, the narrower leaves sometimes lanceolate, obtuse, narrowed at the base, with the midrib and lateral veins prominent beneath, distinct above, glabrous or very sparsely pilose, especially on the midrib and veins. *Peduncle* 11-16 cm. long, terete, pilose, naked below, but with 2 opposite leaves above. *Inflorescence* 5-8 cm. long, 1·7-2·2 cm. in diameter, more or less 4-angled. *Bracts* 2·5 cm. long, 1·8 cm. broad, obovate, shortly aristate, with 4-7 long teeth on the margins, ciliate-glandular on both sides; bracteoles two, 2·5 cm. long, 2 mm. broad, linear, acuminate, acute, glandular. *Sepals* 5; the lateral sepals 5 mm. long, 1·5 mm. broad, linear, shortly aristate; remainder 9 mm. long, 2·5 mm. broad, oblong, subacuminate, ciliate above. *Corolla-tube* 2·2 cm. long, cylindric, ventricose at the base, inflated and glandular above; lobe 1·2 cm. long, 2·2 cm. broad, somewhat semicircular in outline. *Anthers* hairy. *Ovary* 1 cm. long, 3 mm. broad, oblong in outline, shortly beaked, glabrous; style threadlike; stigma inflated and hollow at the apex. *Ovules* 2 in each cell, discoid, covered with scales.

PLATE 77.—Fig. 1, corolla; Fig. 2, a single flower, showing bract and bracteoles; Fig. 3, corolla laid open; Fig. 4, calyx surrounding the ovary; Fig. 5, gynaecium; Fig. 6, apex of style; Fig. 7, ovary with two ovules.

F.P.S.A., 1922.

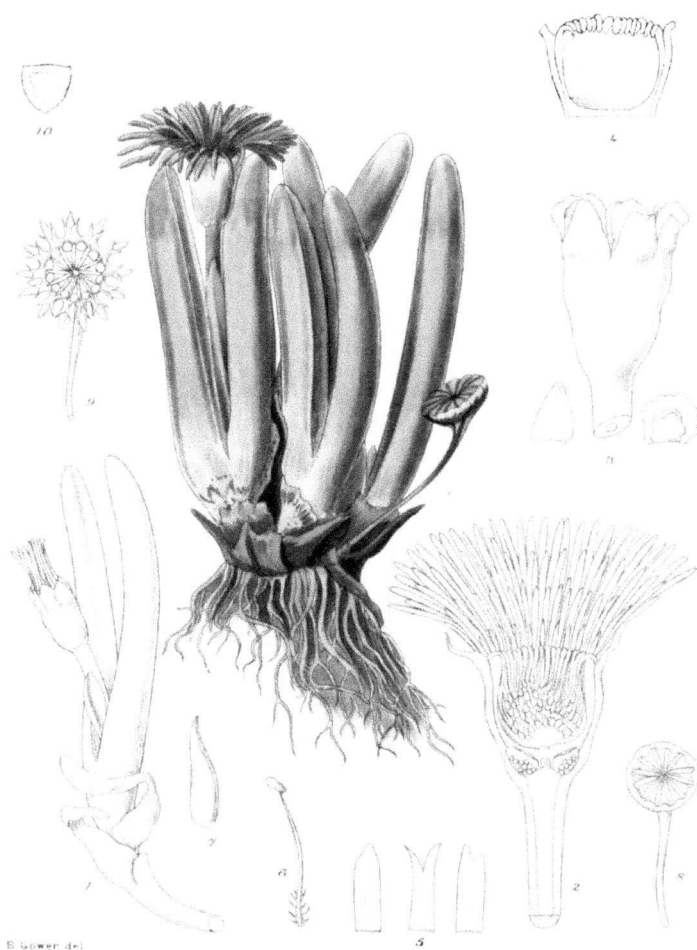

S. GOWER DEL.

PLATE 78.

FICOIDEAE. TRIBE MESEMBRYEAE.

Roodia, *N. E. Brown* (genus novum). *Herba* succulenta, nana, caespitosa. *Proles* bifoliatae. *Pedunculus* bracteatus, uniflorus. *Calyx* in tubum distinctum supra ovarium productus 6-lobus. *Petala* numerosa, libera. *Stamina* numerosissima, pluriseriata, omnia a basi in tubum abrupte inflexa, exterioribus brevioribus. *Ovarium* multiloculare. *Stigma* parvum, inconspicuum, sessile, integrum. *Fructus* multilocularis; loculi alis binis subchartaceis tecti et dorsum versus tuberculo clausi.

Roodia digitifolia, *N. E. Brown. Planta* 8-11 cm. alta, caespitosa, glabra. *Proles* bifoliatae, confertae. *Folia* erecta, 8-11 cm. longa, 10-15 mm. crassa, digitiformia, subteretia faciebus interioribus planis, apice obtusissima, inferne viridia, superne purpureo-tincta. *Pedunculus* 3-6 cm. longus, apice 4-5 mm. crassus, erectus, uniflorus, infra medium bibracteatus, purpureus. *Calycis tubus* cum ovario 10 mm. longus, 10-11 mm. diametro; lobi inaequales, 5-8 mm. longi, 5-7 mm. lati, ovati, obtusi vel subacuti. *Corolla* circiter 4 cm. diametro; petala numerosa, subquadriseriata, exteriora circiter 15 mm. longa et 1 mm. lata, interiora breviora, linearia, apice obtusa vel dentata, pulchre purpurea. *Stamina* numerosissima, in tubum calycis abrupte et arcte inflexa. *Ovarium* supra concavum. *Stigma* sessile, parvum, inconspicuum. *Fructus* 12-14-locularis.

Cape Province: Van Rhynsdorp Division, near Van Rhynsdorp (*Mrs. E. Rood*). Growing at the Division of Botany, Pretoria (Garden No. 403).

This interesting plant is so like some species of *Mesembryanthemum* in general appearance, that most would unhesitatingly place it in that genus. For a long time past, however, as I have elsewhere stated, it has been dawning upon me that *Mesembryanthemum*, as at present understood, is rather of the nature of a natural order than of a single genus. In vegetative characters it presents a very great amount of variation, and in most cases any particular kind of variation is found to be common to several species, so as to form of them a group, indicating a generic difference from the others. About a hundred years ago Haworth recognised this and gave generic names to some of the groups he had formed, which have neither been accepted nor taken notice of by subsequent authors.

Undoubtedly there is a great similarity in the flowers of many groups of this genus that differ widely in their vegetative characteristics; yet when investigated differences in floral structure may often be found also, which, taken in conjunction with vegetative characters, are quite as great and as distinctive as those which separate genera in many other families of plants. This is the case with the plant at present under consideration, for I find that it has a combination of three floral characters, which, so far as known to me do not all occur together in any species of *Mesembryanthemum*, namely: (1) the calyx is produced into a distinct green tube above the ovary; (2) the stamens are all abruptly bent down into the calyx-tube; and (3) the stigma is sessile, undivided, and inconspicuous. Upon this combination of characters in conjunction with its vegetative character, I establish a new genus, and have much pleasure in naming it after its discoverer, Mrs. E. Rood, of Van Rhynsdorp, who sent living plants of it to Dr. I. B. Pole Evans at Pretoria, where it flowered. The accompanying figure of it was sent to me by Dr. Pole Evans, together with a living plant and a flower in fluid, with some notes by Dr. E. P. Phillips, from which the description has been prepared.

DESCRIPTION:—A dwarf succulent plant branching at or below ground level and forming clumps about 8-11 cm. high. *Leaves* 2 to each growth, or 4 when the new growth is made, 8-11 cm. long, 10-15 mm. thick, erect, nearly cylindric or finger-like, but with the inner face flattened, united at the base, obtuse at the apex, glabrous and smooth, green below, purplish at the apical part. *Peduncle* erect, 3-6 cm. long, and 4-5 mm. thick at the apex, with a pair of bracts about 2 cm. long below the middle. *Calyx* 6-lobed, tube (including the ovary) 10 mm. long, produced about 7 mm. above the ovary, about 10-11 mm. in diameter, slightly constricted under the lobes, glabrous, green; lobes unequal, 5-8 mm. long, 5-7 mm. broad, ovate, subacute or obtuse, four of them with membranous margins. *Corolla* about 4 cm. in diameter, petals numerous, in about 4 series, loosely recurved, spreading over one another, the outer about 15 mm. long and 1 mm. broad, the others gradually shorter, all linear, obtuse or notched at the apex, bright magenta. *Stamens* very numerous, all abruptly bent into and closely pressed against the calyx-tube in a dense mass, leaving a clear central opening to the stigma, the outermost series being the shortest. *Stigma* sessile, sunk in a slight pit and level with the concave top of the ovary, entire, inconspicuous.

It may not be out of place to point out that dried specimens of *Mesembryanthemum chrysoleucum*, Schlechter are so similar to *Roodia digitifolia* in general appearance, that the plant might easily be mistaken for a species of *Roodia*. It differs, however, by being destitute of bracts on its peduncle; by the leaves, peduncle, and calyx being papillate; by the calyx being lobed down to the top of the ovary, the stamens erect; and by having 7 stigmas and a 7-celled capsule.—N. E. Brown.

PLATE 78.—Fig. 1, plant 2/3 nat. size; Fig. 2, longitudinal section through the flower; Fig. 3, calyx with 2 sepals; Fig. 4, longitudinal section through receptacle; Fig. 5, petals; Fig. 6, stamen; Fig. 7, bract; Fig. 8, fruit closed; Fig. 9, fruit open; Fig. 10, cross-section of leaf.

F.P.S.A., 1922.

S. GOWER DEL.

PLATE 79.

BAUHINIA Galpinii.

Transvaal.

Leguminosae. Tribe Bauhinieae.

Bauhinia, Linn.; Benth. et Hook. f. Gen. Plant.
Bauhinia Galpinii, *N. E. Br. in Gard. Chron.*

This handsome *Bauhinia*, known in the Transvaal as "The Pride of de Kaap," is a common plant in the low veld east of the Drakensberg. It is a low half-climbing bush, and when in flower is a striking object in the veld, the bright red flowers standing out in sharp contrast to the surrounding vegetation. Specimens were first sent to Kew in 1880 by Mr. T. Nelson, and later Mr. E. E. Galpin sent material which he collected at Barberton. The plant lends itself to cultivation, and may be kept as a trimmed bush in lawns, etc. If left to grow unchecked it becomes very lanky. Our plate was prepared from a specimen growing in the garden of the Division of Botany, Pretoria, and the plant has grown to a height of about 30 ft. up a tree of *Cupressus sempervirens*, var. *pyramidalis*. In cultivation, at least in Pretoria, very few seeds are produced. Specimens are preserved in the National Herbarium, Pretoria (Herb. No. 1601).

DESCRIPTION:—A half-climbing shrub, growing to a height of 5-30 ft. *Branches* with light-brown bark, minutely pubescent. *Leaves* petioled; lamina 1-3 cm. long, 3-5.5 cm. broad, more or less reniform in outline, lobed above, subcordate at the base, with the veining distinct above and prominent beneath, glabrous; petioles

8-1·5 cm. long, convex beneath, channelled above. *Stipules* 3 mm. long, deciduous. *Flowers* in 3-7-flowered racemes opposite the leaves. *Bracts* and bracteoles 3 mm. long, setaceous, deciduous. *Buds* light brown, acuminate, pubescent. *Calyx-tube*, 2-2·7 cm. long; limb spathaceous, unilateral in open flowers. *Petals* long clawed; claws 2 cm. long, somewhat compressed; limb 1·7-2 cm. long, 1·5-1·7 cm. broad, ovate, apiculate, subcordate, at the base. *Fertile stamens* 4; filaments 2·5 cm. long, terete, bent inwards above; anthers 7 mm. long, linear. *Staminodes* 5 mm. long, setaceous, sometimes deeply 2-lobed. *Ovary* on a long gynophore 1·5 cm. long, silky pubescent; style 5 mm. long, stigma capitate. *Fruit* 12·5 cm. long, 2·5 cm. broad, with a double margin along one edge, oblanceolate, tipped with the persistent style, and narrowed at the base. *Seeds* 1·9 cm. long, oblong, flattened, dark brown.

PLATE 79.—Fig. 1, surface view of flower to show staminodes, the limb of the petals removed; Fig. 2, pistil, showing long gynophore; Fig. 3, stamen; Figs. 4, 5, front and side views of calyx; Fig. 6, fruit.

F.P.S.A., 1922.

S. GOWER DEL.

PLATE 80.

KLATTIA Stokoei.
Cape Province.

Iridaceae. Tribe Sisyrinchieae.

Klattia, B. Kr.; Benth. et Hook. f. Gen. Plant.
Klattia Stokoei, *L. Guthrie in Annals Bolus Herb.*

The discovery of this remarkable plant by Mr. T. P. Stokoe on the Hottentot's Holland Mountains, near Somerset West, adds another species to one of the South African endemic genera, which hitherto has been regarded as monotypic. *Klattia partita*, found by Bowie, Thunberg, and Burchell, is a rare plant, and is only known from the Langebergen near Swellendam. It is figured by Marloth in "The Flora of South Africa," t. 41. Our present species differs from *K. partita* in the more spreading leaves, the very much shorter perianth-tube, the narrower segments which have a red limb, and the larger capsule. The genus *Klattia* is closely related to *Witsenia*, which we figured on plate 34, but is distinguished from this genus by having a very short perianth-tube and long segments, much longer than the tube. *Klattia* was named in honour of Dr. F. W. Klatt, a teacher at Hamburg, who published several memoirs on the *Iridaceae*.

Specimens are preserved in the National Herbarium, Pretoria (Herb. No. 1436).

Description:—*Inflorescence* about 8-flowered. *Spathe-valves* 2; the larger 11·5 cm. long, 1 cm. broad, green and lanceolate above, red and strongly keeled below, subacute, glabrous; the smaller red 5 mm. long, 2 mm. broad, rounded above, keeled on the back with the keel produced into a beak 7 mm. long. *Floral* bracts white 3 cm. long, keeled, acute. *Perianth-segments* divided almost to the base 5·7 cm. long, filiform below, broadened above into a linear portion 1 mm. broad. *Filaments* 4·5 mm. long, filiform; anthers 1 mm. long, linear, sagittate at the base. *Ovary* 2 mm. long, 2 mm. in diameter, obovate in outline. Style 6 cm. long, filiform; stigma simple. *Capsule* 1·3 cm. long. *Seeds* 8 mm. long, 2 mm. broad, linear, concave in front, silky and 2-grooved at the back.

PLATE 80.—Fig. 1, portion of stem; Fig. 2, inflorescence; Figs. 3, 4, spathe valves; Fig. 5, a single flower laid open; Fig. 6, pistil; Fig. 7, anther; Fig. 8, ovary; Fig. 9, top of style, showing the three stigmas.

F.P.S.A., 1922.

I. B. Pole Evans

INDEX TO VOLUME II.

www.ingramcontent.com/pod-product-compliance
Lightning Source LLC
LaVergne TN
LVHW021513080426
835509LV00018B/2497